Contents

Foreword

What is it that adds sparkle and life to a well-planned and implemented public relations campaign? It's the 'ah' factor: that brilliantly simple, but inspired creative edge.

When it comes to decision time for the internal or external client and all other things are equal, being creative (note this does not equal wacky) usually wins the day.

Creativity is a gift most of us desire, but only a few seem to have. However, help is at hand, because this book demonstrates that creativity is not just the privilege of the lucky few, but can be the practice for us all. Yes, it is possible to learn to be creative, but as with all public relations techniques and skills, it takes work and effort to develop.

In this third edition of the world's first book on creativity in public relations, Andy Green debunks some of the myths surrounding creativity and then carefully and thoroughly takes us through the five 'I's of the creative process. He introduces the notion of a disciplined approach to creative thinking and gives practical advice on how to evaluate creative ideas. Summarizing some of the obstacles that impede the creative process, Andy then goes on to describe how both individuals and organizations can release their creativity.

An insightful and interesting chapter on 'Impropaganda' explores the role of the publicist as opposed to the public relations professional and encourages us to define more clearly the boundaries of what is acceptable in the name of creativity.

Finally, the author looks at the future of creativity and the tools that can be developed to help public relations professionals to enhance and enliven their work.

A helpful endpiece giving details of courses, books and other sources of information on creativity rounds off the profession's only book on the subject.

As Andy Green says, the book is designed to 'improve your creative abilities, manage the creative dimension and understand the creative process'. It does that in a thorough and practical way. It's a book that should be on every practitioner's shelf and it should be read and referenced regularly to stimulate the grey cells and to provide a route-map to lively, engaging and realistic public relations programmes.

Anne Gregory
Series Editor

Acknowledgements

Research interviews were gratefully conducted with the following leading individuals in the PR field. Unless otherwise stated, quotations in this book attributed to these people arose during my interviews with them. They are:

Mark Borkowski, Creative Director, Mark Borkowski Press and PR.
Paul Carroll, Chief Executive, Communique Public Relations.
Max Clifford, Director, Max Clifford and Associates.
Gordon Forbes, Managing Director, Ptarmigan Public Relations.
Steve Gebbett, Creative Director, Charles Barker BSMG.
Graham Lancaster, Chairman, Biss Lancaster.
Alan Preece, Director of Communications, University of East Anglia.

Additional copy-editing: Harvey Smith.

Beta readers: Judith Barber, Jim Britton, Simon Clark, Helen Kettleborough, Steve McDermott, David Marsh, and Harvey Smith.

Thanks to Tony Murray, editor of *Adline*, for telling me about the two tribes in public relations; Dawn Boswell, David Holmes, and Douglas Smith for their additional creative soundbites.

Series Editor: Anne Gregory.

Thanks to the authors quoted for kind permission to reproduce extracts from their books.

PR in Practice Series

Published in association with the Chartered Institute of Public Relations
Series Editor: Anne Gregory

Kogan Page has joined forces with the Chartered Institute of Public Relations to publish this unique series, which is designed specifically to meet the needs of the increasing numbers of people seeking to enter the public relations profession and the large band of existing PR professionals. Taking a practical, action-oriented approach, the books in the series concentrate on the day-to-day issues of public relations practice and management rather than academic history. They provide ideal primers for all those on CIPR, CAM and CIM courses or those taking NVQs in PR. For PR practitioners, they provide useful refreshers and ensure that their knowledge and skills are kept up to date.

Anne Gregory is one of the UK's leading public relations academics. She is Director of the Centre for Public Relations Studies at Leeds Business School, a faculty of Leeds Metropolitan University. Before becoming an academic, Anne spent 12 years in public relations practice and has experience at a senior level both in-house and in consultancy. She remains involved in consultancy work and is a non-executive director of South West Yorkshire Mental Health NHS Trust with special responsibility for financial and communication issues. Anne is Consultant Editor of the PR in Practice series and edited the book of the same name and wrote *Planning and Managing Public Relations Campaigns*, also in this series. She was President of the CIPR in 2004.

Other titles in the series:
Effective Internal Communication by Lyn Smith and Pamela Mounter
Effective Personal Communication Skills by Andy Green
Effective Writing Skills for PR by John Foster
Managing Activism by Denise Deegan
Online Public Relations by David Phillips
Planning and Managing Public Relations Campaigns by Anne Gregory
Public Affairs in Practice by Stuart Thompson and Dr Steve John
Public Relations: A practical guide to the basics by Philip Henslowe
Public Relations in Practice edited by Anne Gregory
Public Relations Strategy by Sandra Oliver
Risk Issues and Crisis Management in Public Relations by Michael Regester and Judy Larkin
Running a Public Relations Department by Mike Beard

The above titles are available from all good bookshops. To obtain further information, please go to the CIPR website (www.cipr.co.uk/books) or contact the publishers at the address below:

Kogan Page Limited
120 Pentonville Road
London N1 9JN
Tel: 020 7278 0433 Fax: 020 7837 6348
www.kogan-page.co.uk

Introduction

The subject of creativity in public relations is something of an enigma. Ask any client or senior manager what key skills are required by a PR practitioner and they will invariably include the ability to be creative and to add the creative dimension to their work.

In the UK, public relations practitioners work in an industry with millions of pounds spent by organizations and clients to pay them to be creative and practise creativity. The industry also has a well-established series of professional awards, where individual programmes of work are praised (more often than not) for their creativity. Often the creative dimension is considered the crucial element.

Yet when it comes to studying the subject of creativity in public relations, there are no books about it, or even chapters within textbooks, and usually not even an index reference.

Creativity in Public Relations attempts to fill this lacuna. It is written to help public relations practitioners understand the creative process – both how it works and how it can be managed. It also explains how public relations practitioners can improve their own individual creative skills, using and managing a range of techniques and tips to generate creative ideas.

This book is focused on the needs of public relations practitioners and includes practical examples from the author's career in public relations, spanning more than 25 years, as well as research among many of the leading figures in the industry who are regarded by their peers as 'creative'. See Figure 0.1 for some idea of the areas that will be covered.

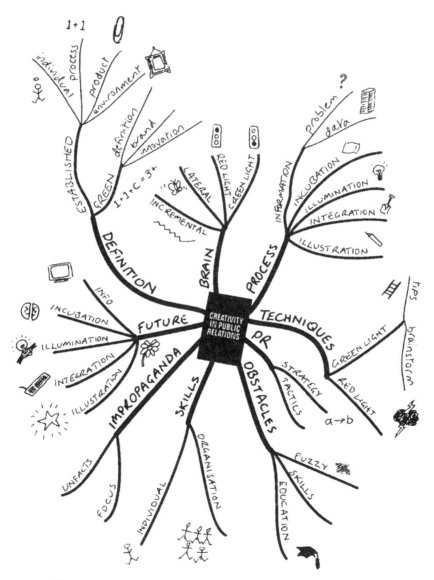

Figure 0.1 *A mind map of this book and its contents*
(See page 81 for more on mind maps.)

This is not a catalogue of creative ideas, although there are many examples of outstanding creative work. Rather, the idea is to help practitioners 'get under the skin of creativity' to use it to greater effect in their work and in wider aspects of their lives.

As Alex Osborn, one of the great pioneers of creative thinking, observed: 'Far too many people are leading their lives like they're driving their cars with the brakes on.' This book will enable you to take your foot off that brake pedal.

1

A definition of 'creativity'

This is very creative, but...

An anonymous client

Far too often the word 'creative' in public relations is used to describe the off-beat, the irreverent and, at times, the downright silly. This 'creative' activity can be likened to the experience of actress Maureen Lipman when staying in a hotel. There was a knock on the door while she was in the shower. 'Hello, I have a telegram for you', said the porter. 'Can you slip it under the door?' replied Ms Lipman. 'No, I can't,' replied the porter, 'it's on a tray.' Rather like the porter's tray, so much of what constitutes 'creativity' in public relations practice actually gets in the way of delivering the message.

One of the goals set for this book is to establish a definition of 'creativity' that is readily understandable, memorable and relevant for your work. This understanding of 'creativity' will help you analyse any activity that you are likely to meet in your work, and so make you a truly creative public relations practitioner.

SOME POSSIBLE DEFINITIONS

The word 'creativity' is not only widely used – indeed abused – but also seems to have 1,001 different definitions. Creativity is one of those things much easier to detect than to define. Such definitions fall into one or more of these categories:

- as an individual talent;
- as a process;
- as a product; and
- as recognition by others;

each of which is explored further below.

Creativity as an individual talent

The poet William Wordsworth captured the spirit of creativity being an individual talent when he wrote of inspiration as 'the flash upon the inward eye'. Many of us can relate to moments when an idea for a photocall or a campaign sprang forward in our imagination. These ideas seemingly came from nowhere and appeared to be the product solely of our brain. The essence of this definition is seeing 'creativity' as an innate individual talent.

Facing the task of developing our own working definition of 'creativity' for public relations practitioners, if we were to use just this definition then a tautology emerges: 'Creativity is what creative people do'. This is clearly insufficient for our purpose; if we all have this creative ability, what marks out work regarded as 'creative' from that seen as 'non-creative'?

Creativity as a process

The process of 'creativity' has also been used as a definition. The writer Arthur Koestler characterized creativity as 'two disconnected notions accidentally coming together'. The mechanics of how creative ideas are produced is used as a definition.

It is certainly true that the bringing together of different elements creates something new. Yet, as we shall see, the outstanding creative idea springs from many not-so-good ideas – a result of the same process of combining different elements. The

5

bringing together of disconnected notions may be the raw material of creating ideas, but it does not automatically equate with generating 'creative ideas'.

So while the process of creativity is important, it is not by itself adequate to serve as a definition.

Creativity as a product

Ask most people what they think of as 'creativity' and, more often than not, the answer will be works of art or great achievements. In my lectures on creativity, a paper clip and a painting by Magritte are held up before the audience and the question posed: 'Which is the more creative?' Invariably Magritte wins; my response is that we take paper clips for granted. Although our society may place different cultural values on the relative merits of a paper clip and a painting, in fact they are equally creative. They each offer 'added value' in their respective tasks. The paper clip is an ingenious way of twisting a small thin piece of metal to provide a device to hold different sheets of paper together; the painting offers an opportunity for a fellow human being to provide a new insight into the world in which we live.

The use of 'creativity' in some form of problem solving is an important facet of the creative act, whether it is looking at holding papers together or producing what is judged as 'art'. In establishing a suitable definition of 'creativity', the product and the value produced by the creative work are clearly important. Yet there is still a need to look at the wider context of the creative act.

Creativity as recognition by others

As a proud parent, I shared in the feeling of achievement when my daughter Charlotte came home from nursery with one of her first paintings. To me it was a tremendous piece of 'creativity': my little girl had done this! But to anyone else it would probably be – and I do not mean to denigrate Charlotte's talents in any way – a piece of immature, technically undeveloped artistic work. Although I might similarly obtain a great deal of pleasure from the work of, say, Magritte (one of my favourite artists), his work has a far more universal appeal and value as a creative product than my daughter's.

This recognition by a wider audience is seen by some as a crucial element in defining 'creativity'. The creative process is not only at the point of origination with the creator but also in its recognition by others, where they in turn may need to demonstrate creative skills and understanding to appreciate and value the work of creativity. In the example of the artist, it is not enough for him to be creative, but the audience has to be creative in recognizing the creative qualities of the work.

One of the world's leading experts on the subject of creativity, Professor Morris Stein, told me his definition of creativity in a conversation: 'Creativity is a process that results in novelty which is accepted as useful, tenable or satisfying by a significant group of others at some point in time'. By 'significant group of others' he means those who have influence or power to determine what is recognized as of value in a group. In a public relations context, 'significant others' could be defined as fellow practitioners, or users and consumers of our product or service, such as journalists and clients.

There is still an element of tautology in this approach, where it is saying: 'Creativity is what people, who have been recognized as "creative", do'. Nonetheless, its emphasis on *placing value, and identifying a cultural context*, is an important step in developing our own working definition of 'creativity' for public relations practitioners.

A TIME AND A PLACE

Invariably, as soon as someone in the business hears about my interest in creativity, they give me the line: 'Well you know there's no such thing as a new idea in public relations. It's all been done before'. My considered response is: 'Yes, you're partly right. Many combinations of different elements have been used widely in the past'. There are also practitioners who dismiss the efforts of their colleagues who, they claim, have 'stolen' ideas that have been used before – they regard these efforts at being creative as somehow almost fraudulent.

There is a metaphor of great insight from the Greek philosopher Heraclitus, who argued that 'A man never stands in the same river twice'. When faced with the task of being creative, we are in a world that, like a river, is constantly changing. Consequently it is

perfectly legitimate – and, indeed, creative – to use an idea that has previously been employed, because the context will be different and the world has moved on in some way.

There are numerous examples of ideas seemingly ahead of their time. The reality is often that the combination of elements could not produce added value at the time the ideas were presented. With a change in context, perhaps with other technological, social or historical developments, the added-value element can be achieved in a different context. Leonardo da Vinci produced designs for a helicopter, which could only be brought to fruition when advances in other fields of technology and aeronautics could make human flight a reality. In similar fashion, there is nothing wrong in 'stealing' other people's ideas; the context in which the ideas are later used is the important point. However, when it comes to presenting these ideas as your own, that is a matter between you, your conscience, and the availability of evidence of the original idea.

A DEFINITION FOR PUBLIC RELATIONS PRACTITIONERS

Public relations work creates or manages change. A working definition of creativity must contain some form of process and end product. Furthermore, public relations is a dynamic process in operation within the wider society, and so some reference to its context should also be made.

By examining these different approaches to defining creativity, a working definition for public relations practitioners can be given. Thus:

Creativity is the ability each of us has to create something new by bringing together two or more different elements in a new context, in order to provide added value to a task.

A creative act consists of not only originating but also evaluating the added value it contributes. It is not novelty for its own sake, but it must produce some form of value that can be recognized by a third party.

As a mathematical sum it could read $1 + 1 + C = 3+$;

where 1 equals an element to be used in the creative process and C = creativity. By introducing the creative dimension, practitioners can produce a new synergy so as to achieve greater value than the individual component parts.

To elaborate on what is meant by bringing together different elements to create a synergy to provide added value, Table 1.1 gives some simple examples.

Table 1.1 *Combining elements to provide added value*

Area of work	First element	Second element	Added value
Artist – creating a new painting.	Raw materials: paint, canvas. The subject matter.	Individual vision, craft and skill in creating images.	An image that may bring pleasure or new insight into the world.
Poet – creating a new verse.	Raw materials: pen, paper. The subject matter.	Individual vision, craft and skill in using language.	A text that may bring pleasure or new insight into the world.
Public relations professional – devising a photocall.	The subject matter. Props to use in the photograph.	Person or celebrity to use in the photograph.	Extra media coverage and a visual dramatization of a story.

In a nutshell, creativity can be summarized as: 'flexible thinking around beautiful quetions, in quest for added value.'

ADDED VALUE

An editor of a marketing magazine once remarked to me: 'As far as I can see, there are two types of public relations people: those whose immediate reaction is to say "What creative thing can we do?"; and those who respond by saying "We don't bother with this creative stuff. We just get on with the nuts and bolts of a story or campaign."' My reply was swift: 'They are both wrong.'

The public relations profession can be divided into three tribes. Some practitioners may be members of the 'dash-off-into-dottiness brigade' – those who instantly propose an offbeat idea before considering any real need for the end product. Or they may be members of the second, 'nuts-and-bolts tribe' – those who decide not to be creative and seemingly fail to exploit the full potential of an opportunity. Third, there is a growing number of the 'added-value connoisseurs'. The mark of an outstanding creative practitioner is to analyse the situation coolly and to assess what is required – and only then, crucially, to decide what added value is needed.

Here is an example of what demonstrates the role of 'added value' in public relations work. In the early 1990s I helped win a major account: the launch of a major aluminium can recycling scheme across the UK. The client, unhappy with the low level of media coverage it was receiving, was looking for an agency that was 'creative'. In our proposals we came up with all sorts of what we thought were wonderfully creative ideas, such as having pop star Gary Glitter jumping out of giant cans, despite which we still managed to win the account! (Ten years later, the pop star was convicted of possessing child pornography – an example of the impact a 'new context' can have on a creative product.)

However, we were surprised by the fact that the company was getting disappointing coverage. The campaign was at a time when the environment was emerging as a major public issue so that interest in all things 'green' was very topical, and the company was launching a new recycling concept of paying for items to be recycled (in contrast with other schemes that merely involved leaving your items in the recycling bin). This, we felt, had a very strong news interest and should get media coverage without the need for gimmicks.

Once we had won the account, close inspection of the company's previous press release material revealed why it was not getting adequate media coverage. The reason was not that the company was being uncreative, but because its news releases were, in our view, badly written. In reality, like the porter's tray in Maureen Lipman's story, they were getting in the way of the message. All that was necessary to achieve the desired result was to produce well-written material that conveyed the news of the story clearly. There was no requirement for 'added value' from the creative function.

 Pause for a moment. Reflect back on your own work. Try and identify examples of 'added value' from your creative contribution to a situation.

Who decides what is added value?

If creativity is adding value, who decides the measure of the added value? The answer lies in the context of the creative act. In the context of my daughter Charlotte's family, her picture provided added value in the eyes of her parents; knowing the skills of their child, the new work of art provided added value as evidence of her growing development and talents. In a wider context, the picture may have very little added value: another painting by a child, which in the eyes of a dispassionate observer has provided no new insights. The same work of art has a different value in different contexts.

The examples of a public relations practitioner producing a press release reveals how the added value within a creative piece of work can vary according to its context. Here are three different contexts to illustrate the point:

- *Context 1: the PR agency.* The draft release presented for approval to a senior manager or client may appear to have added value as a result of some creative element within it. In this example, the practitioners may have previously had problems getting material approved for being regarded as insufficiently creative. They now regard their new work as truly creative, because its added value has enabled them to achieve a key objective – in this instance, that of providing their abilities to their manager or client.
- *Context 2: overloaded media.* When the news release is subsequently issued to the media, the story may bomb, perhaps as a result of a large number of other major news stories at the same time. The creative element inherent in the news release may appear to have had insufficient added value, as it failed to be used by its target, the media.
- *Context 3: underused media.* Maybe a year later, exactly the same news story could be updated and reissued at a quiet news time. As a result, it may achieve extensive coverage. In this new context the added value may appear quite significant. It is exactly the same creative product, but in a different context. Its

value has varied considerably according to the different context.

The subsequent worth of added value is determined by the impact of the creative product on its marketplace, and the relative importance of that marketplace in the wider society. The added value will subsequently be affected by time and a shifting context.

Added value is a form of currency. Despite the best efforts of the creative practitioners, the measure of the added value in any creative work is evaluated externally to the creator. Like a currency, their creative product may be devalued by issues beyond their control.

Creative people can, however, act like the currency speculator identifying which currencies are currently valuable and which are likely to change in value. They can then produce work in relation to potential value and aim to capitalize on the most opportune external factors. But they cannot dictate the actual value of their creative product; although they may be able to place a commercial price tag on their work, the qualitative evaluation by others of the creative product is beyond their power. At best, creative people may influence how the added value is perceived in their respective markets, yet cannot control the outside world.

By understanding that creative products must offer added value, and appreciating that the measure of the added value may vary, depending on the context it is presented within, creative practitioners can at least seek to maximize the creative value of their work. They may recognize that some contexts will be more lucrative than others.

THE CONTEXT FOR CREATIVITY

Although a definition of 'creativity' has been established, it is important to put this into the context within which practitioners perform their skills. Artists have the freedom, if they wish, to make whatever statement they want in their creative work. Creative public relations practitioners do not have this luxury – a position best explained by a story from my early days in the profession.

My first job in public relations was in local government. During this time I came across Councillor Jack Brown. Now, Jack's heart was in the right place and I have a lot of respect for how, in his

proper job in adult education, he helped unemployed working-class kids get on in life. However, Jack was known to hit the head-lines frequently in the local press. The episode I most vividly recall is the time he got a young nude female model holding a bowl of fruit to stand outside a Job Centre to promote adult education classes.

In this book we will examine a number of techniques, such as focusing to identify what is at the heart of a story or issue, or suspending judgement when considering potential ideas. Technically, Jack was absolutely correct in his reading of the situation, asking himself: 'How can I get a group of unemployed people who think education is boring, and not relevant to them, interested in adult education classes?' His analysis crystallized the idea of what he was offering people in adult education as providing the fruits of knowledge. He then presumably posed a further question: 'How can I demonstrate these "fruits of knowledge" and make this interesting to the newspapers (ie give the publicity "added value")?' Hence, Jack arrived at the idea of the nude woman with the fruit bowl standing outside the Job Centre...

The idea initially achieved extensive press coverage, with the bowl of fruit placed in a strategic position for family newspapers, and further coverage of the subsequent row from fellow Labour councillors about exploitation of women.

On one level this was a seemingly brilliant piece of tactical creative public relations achieving significant 'added value' in terms of extra coverage. Later in this book the subject of 'Impropaganda' will be examined as a creative tactic. However, the profound shortcoming of Jack's publicity stunt was that it compromised the brand values of his organization. Every outstanding creative practitioner interviewed in the research for this book stresses how any creative act must not compromise the brand and its inherent values.

The creative function can be employed to extend or create new organizational or brand values. But creativity is bringing out qualities or issues inherent within the organization. Any fool can get publicity (and I am not calling Cllr Jack Brown a fool by any means), but the mark of the creative public relations practitioner is to achieve this without compromising the brand or organizational values.

The public relations practitioner can fall foul of an organization, not fully recognizing its values or where and when they can be

compromised. An example is when one of the UK's most outstanding creative practitioners, Mark Borkowski, launched an alcopop product named 'Thickhead' in 1997. As Mark takes up the story:

> It was a classic case where we came up with a very creative campaign – we even came up with some advertising straplines for it. But we didn't understand the process inside the client, a brewery, who had given the go-ahead to some bright young things within the company to go up and create this brand. No one seriously considered the impact. And because of the type of PR they always got, no one expected [the product] to explode in such a way that [it] provoked strong parliamentary and pressure group reaction to the idea of encouraging young people to drink. They had no fabric of actually dealing with it at a high level, so the immediate reaction was to kick it into touch. It was a case of 'Give me dangerous radio'. But when you are given 'dangerous radio' or creative PR, the client has to actually know what they are dealing with.

Reflecting back, Mark adds:

> A failure on our part was to really drive home and make sure people within the organization fully understood what they were getting involved with. If you don't set the ground properly, and get all the details in place with your clients – so they can understand them – then you can have a creative failure on your hands.

 Consider whether you know of any examples from your own work, or elsewhere, where an organization's brand values have been compromised by a so-called creative public relations activity.

CREATIVITY VERSUS INNOVATION

As this is a public relations study on the subject of 'creativity', it is only right there should be some public relations effort to create greater understanding on behalf of the subject of 'creativity' itself. For many, the word 'creativity' has what may be called a touchy-feely nature to it, not really suitable for the hard world of business. Yet, mention the word 'innovation' and suddenly the act of creating new ideas takes on a more credible resonance in certain quarters, such as the business media and various government-backed development agencies.

Professor Simon Majaro of Cranfield School of Management defines innovation in this manner in his book *Managing Ideas for Profit* (Majaro, 1992): 'Creativity is the thinking process that helps us generate ideas. Innovation is the practical application of such ideas towards meeting the organization's objectives in a more effective way.' But this means all ideas are creative. In reality, many ideas will be rejected. Using the working definition of creativity put forward in this book, to be 'creative' the idea must offer some form of added value. Also, creativity is not just a means of coming up with ideas, but actually has a far wider meaning – which will be highlighted in the study of the creative process in Chapter 4.

Innovation can instead be defined as *'the adoption, adaptation, or implementation by a third party of someone's creativity (ie an added-value product)'*. When appraising a painting, one does not say: 'The artist is being innovative'. Should another artist adopt some element of this work, such as its style, subject matter, materials or techniques used, then the original work can be said to be innovative; it has inspired the application of some creative element of the original work by a third party.

CREATIVE THINKING VERSUS NON-CREATIVE THINKING

What is the difference between creative thinking and non-creative thinking? The answer is 'None'. They both use the same mechanics of combining different elements to create something new. It's the value achieved that differentiates them.

When the great British snack of baked beans on toast was first made, it was an example of creative cookery. A chef somewhere recognized the potential in combining a serving of baked beans with a slice of toasted bread. Now, however, the snack has been eaten a countless number of times, and it has long ceased to be an example of a creative recipe.

Non-creative chefs will make a meal with such a recipe, combining ingredients that have been used before but in the same way. Creative chefs will use the same process of combining different ingredients while displaying originality in their choice of these, making them unusual or distinctive in some way. The way the finished meal is presented, or the context it is served in, also provides opportunities for added value. It is the synergy

15

produced by the creative chef's use of combinations that marks out his or her creativity, not the use of a different form of thinking or the mechanics of combining different elements.

Non-creative thinking combines different elements, but will apply exactly the same combination of elements previously used, without any novelty or significant change in the context in which they are applied. The creative person will display more originality in the sourcing and choice of items to combine, or in their permutation, or in the context in which the combination of elements is used, and may even challenge the context itself. As a result, the creative thinker has the potential to achieve added value – in contrast to the so-called non-creative thinker – but will still use the same mechanics of combining different elements to create something new.

BIG 'C' OR LITTLE 'c'?

Any study of the subject of creativity will sooner or later come across what can be called the 'big "C" or little "c"?' argument. For some, the act of 'creativity' is the preserve of the great artist or practitioner, where only the truly great can be called 'creative'. In the other corner are the advocates of little 'c', believing that creativity is available to all for use in whatever task – whether in art, housework, or filling in your tax return.

Many people in the public relations business employ the convenient cop-out: 'Oh, I haven't got a creative bone in me', and use this as an excuse for not being creative and not taking part fully in group exercises such as brainstorming. Others say: 'You are either creative or you are not'. Practitioners should take heart from the great writer on the advertising scene, Winston Fletcher, who says in his book *How to Capture the Advertising High Ground* (Fletcher, 1994) that creativity 'is like height, weight and strength… we all have differing amounts, but we all have at least some'. Make the best use of your own creative capabilities by understanding the creative process, use the many creative techniques available, and be aware of what influences individual and group creative skills.

It is a fundamental belief underpinning this book that we can all strive to make greater and more effective use of a talent we all possess, and that *we are all creative*.

SUMMARY

1. Creativity has previously been defined as: an individual skill; a process; the product of combining two or more elements; and by the different value placed upon the creative product.
2. There is nothing wrong in borrowing or re-using an idea. All ideas are presented in a new context.
3. Added value is the fundamental element of anything that is defined as creative. The measure of this added value is determined by its context.
4. Creative thinking uses the same mechanisms as non-creative thinking.
5. Innovation is the use by a third party of a creative product.
6. Creative public relations practitioners have to work within brand values.
7. We all have varying degrees of creative talent.

KEY WORDS FOR YOUR CREATIVITY VOCABULARY

- Added value.
- Innovation.
- New context.

2

Creativity: some myths debunked

This lacks the Big Idea.
Words of a prospective client, which changed my life

Understanding the so-called 'Big Ideas', the different types of thinking processes used, and the context of lateral thinking, are crucial to being creative.

THE MYTH OF THE INSTANT 'BIG IDEA'

My inspiration to study the subject of creativity came after submitting what I thought was the perfect pitch document for a prospective client. I felt that it offered the definitive solution to the client's needs, that it was full of good creative ideas relevant to this situation. I was genuinely taken aback by the client's response. He said: 'This lacks the Big Idea'.

Driven by a need to prove the client wrong, I racked my brains for a Big Idea. Nothing came to mind, and neither did the client's

business come our way. But from then on, I wanted to get to the bottom of what made Big Ideas and to study creativity.

Many people seem to think that creativity is producing the Big Idea – an idea from nowhere so clever and so profound that it defines creativity. In public relations work it may be the new campaign idea that no one else has thought of, which will achieve significant publicity, or the photocall gimmick that shows the product in a new light and generates extensive media coverage. One of the key lessons of this book, and a clear message to the prospective client who rejected my proposals, is this: *the instant Big Idea does not exist.*

Creativity, and its task of generating ideas, is essentially incremental. Ideas come through a series of small steps or moves. They build up each other to produce the final idea. Look back on any idea you have come up with; think back to precisely how the idea grew, and trace its lineage. The blinding flash of inspiration will, if you are honest enough, be linked to an earlier idea or element that you may have been dealing with. Rather than the creative idea being an instant revelation, it will more likely be characterized by a haphazard series of moves, steps and linkages.

This incremental nature of creativity is confirmed by the UK's Patent Office, which reports that 95 per cent of new patents are merely adaptations of existing ones. (A study of the remaining 5 per cent of patents would, I suspect, reveal that they are the products of incremental thought.) Any truly great idea (possessing significant added value) will generally have emerged as a result of a series of incremental small steps in generating it, with much of its inherent added value gained in the subsequent implementation, or in how it was sold.

Examine any field of activity where creative ideas are generated and used, whether it is the world of management, the arts, or television comedy. Their ideas are created through a number of mini-steps, not via an instant, earth-shattering moment of inspiration. Indeed, the management guru Tom Peters describes in his book *A Passion for Excellence* (Peters, 1996) several case studies where organizations made decisions to pursue a Big Idea: 'In all of history it seems, from French fry seasoning at McDonald's to IBM's System/360 computer, the first and second prototypes don't work.' Often the key people in a project were simply intent on 'making it work'; through trial and error they eventually succeeded. No Big Idea brought an instant solution.

19

Otto Frederick Rohwedder invented sliced bread in 1912. The machine was a complete failure. It wasn't until 20 years later when a new brand called Wonder started marketing sliced bread that the invention caught on. It wasn't the 'Big idea' or the sheer convenience and innovation of pre-slicing bread, but the packaging and advertising, 'builds strong bodies twelve ways'.

Seth Godin (2005), Purple Cow, *Penguin, London*

Contemporaries of Mozart described him at work as 'taking dictation from God' in the way he seemed to translate a concept in his mind on to paper. Research has, however, showed him to be very meticulous, making changes and additions to his work. Music from a more recent era provides contemporary examples of this incremental process in practice. The Beatles anthology albums offer a fascinating insight into how their ideas developed. The original versions of their songs often bore little resemblance to the final product, then hailed as 'creative masterpieces'. The reality of producing a creative work of art, whether it is in music, painting or writing, is of artists constantly making changes and adding incremental new ideas to their work.

They may appear to the outside world as being able to come up with ideas effortlessly; as creative. In reality however, they are 'unconsciously competent'.

It is not just in the world of art that the incremental process is present. Look at any popular, long-running television show and you will see the evolution of creative ideas at work. The BBC television show *Only Fools and Horses* had a lead character (Del Boy) who is characterized by having outrageously pretentious drinks in the pub. Yet in the early episodes he is seen merely ordering a more mundane half-pint of lager. The writer of the series, John Sullivan, appears to have developed the comic character of Del Boy and his outrageous drinks after he had created the original character – clear evidence of an incremental process at work.

So how has the notion of the Big Idea come about? One explanation may be that, in order for us to be comfortable with the world we inhabit, we like to package things in a neat and orderly way. This includes our understanding of how creative ideas are arrived at. It is much more convenient to believe great creative people somehow intuitively and instantly arrive at Big Ideas rather than recognize that creativity can be a messy, unglamorous and protracted process.

The individual egos of creative people, coupled with the need for journalists and historians to write a story with a clear beginning, middle and end, contribute to perpetuating the myth of the Big Idea. Commenting on this phenomenon, Professor John Jewkes, in his study of famous inventors, 1970, wrote:

> Successful inventors contribute to the romantic aura... It is much more agreeable for them to think of their achievements as the outcome of a flawless chain of brilliant decisions and deliberate planning than as the result of desperate groping and frequent back-tracking... Subsequent writers, possessing more complete records of the lucky strokes than of the numerous failures, and searching for a tidy story rather than a muddled one, carry on the building up of the legends.

A detailed examination of the world's greatest inventions highlights the perpetuation of the myth about the instant Big Idea, masking the reality of the incremental process at work. Ask who invented the steam engine and you will most likely get the answer of James Watt, with the image of the young James sitting in his mother's kitchen being inspired by watching a kettle boil. Yet the reality was of Watt cleverly adapting wider applications for the steam pump, which had been invented earlier by Newcombe; Watt's inspiration came from extending the use of a machine used for pumping water out of coal-mines, not from the vision supplied by a steaming kettle.

Moreover, the actuality of invention reveals that great discoveries were often achieved more by chance than from being the result of someone's Big Idea. Coca-Cola was originally a hangover cure. Dr Marten's boots were originally conceived as orthopaedic shoes for elderly German maidens.

Inventions are perfected by step-by-step improvements, and each step is itself an invention. Paying tribute to this incremental process, Sir Isaac Newton observed: 'If I have seen far, it is because I have stood on the shoulders of giants.' Newton was aware of how he could have made his major discoveries only by incrementally advancing ideas developed by others. Thomas Edison provided valuable guidance for any would-be creative when he recommended: 'Make it a point to keep on the lookout for novel and interesting ideas that others have used successfully. Your idea has to be original only in its adaptation to the problem you are currently working on.'

Some practitioners, keen to uphold the concept of the instant Big Idea, use examples from their own careers as evidence of its existence. Usually what emerges is that they have subconsciously used a technique described in Chapter 5 – the SCAMPER checklist, which encourages you to use a series of 'change' words or phrases. One of these, such as 'to make bigger' or 'to make smaller', is placed against the situation, and the individual then thinks through the consequences of applying this to the task at hand. Invariably, the proponent of the Big Idea has actually employed a technique in response to the question: 'What can I do to make this the biggest idea/event/theme ever?', and comes up with something that is usually big in scale rather than necessarily large in added value – which would be the true criterion of any genuinely Big Idea.

People also confuse Big Ideas with what can instead be called a 'Big Provocation', which challenges the assumptions of an orthodox way of thinking or doing. The writer Tom Peters, for example, is a good example of someone who passionately believes in Big Ideas, yet in reality his writing is describing a process for challenging a mindset, or what is described in Chapter 4 as a 'paradigm of a situation'.

To pose a question that can attack or undermine an assumption is not a creative idea itself. A Big Provocation may set in place a train of thought that can lead to a major added-value idea – this process is essentially incremental rather than being the instant creation of a Big Idea.

Sometimes a 'Big Vision' (see Chapter 13) is confused with a Big Idea. An individual may possess a vision of where in the future they would like to be, or may have a major goal to achieve, such as 'I want to find a cure for cancer'. This may be a Big Vision, as it provides a vivid visual reference point of a desired position, but it is not a Big Idea, as it lacks an added-value combination in a new context to provide a solution to a goal.

Remembering our definition of creativity from Chapter 1, in which a creative idea is defined as a product created from a combination of elements in a new context, it is clear that neither Big Provocation nor Big Vision can be called Big Ideas.

Another cause for confusion is the ideas that come to us seemingly out of the blue. These are often confused with Big Ideas. In reality, they are merely 'illuminations' – the third stage of the creative process described in Chapter 4.

The instant Big Idea – created as an initial illumination, isolated from the task in hand – does not exist, except perhaps in consultancy pitch documents and picture-postcard-sized studies of history. The myth of the instant Big Idea is a fundamental point for public relations practitioners to consider about creativity, for two reasons. First, practitioners work in an environment where their clients or management may at times demand an instant Big Idea for the task in hand. Yet, no idea lives in a vacuum: practitioners will need to educate their peers if they want them to fully understand – and manage – the creative dimension in their work. Second, this book will examine a number of tools and techniques for practical use by public relations practitioners. All of these harness the incremental nature of creativity. If you give yourself the task of thinking up the instant Big Idea, invariably it leads to what I call 'constipated thinking' – the desire for an outcome is there, but little else materializes.

The trick to creativity and creating new ideas is not how you think up the instant Big Idea, but rather what you can do to generate little ideas, which can later be combined in some way to be presented as a Big Idea. The message for anyone seeking an idea is to *think small rather than tall*.

 Think for a moment about episodes in your career where you may have been asked to come up with a Big Idea. In the light of your new knowledge about the myth of the instant Big Idea, consider how you might have approached the task differently.

THE MYTH OF LEFT-BRAIN/RIGHT-BRAIN THEORY

As a result of the work by the Nobel prizewinner Professor Roger Sperry, the theory of right and left sides of the brain was advanced, in which major intellectual functions were split between different parts of the brain. On the left side, it was believed, were the logical, rational and controlling aspects to our thinking, while the right side was said to control our inspirational and creative thoughts. It was argued that different people's skills were linked to the different hemispheres of the brain dominating an individual's performance. More creative people were seemingly right-side

dominated; others who were more analytical but less creative were described as left-side dominated.

However, left-brain/right-brain theory has since been undermined by research that shows mental skills being distributed throughout the brain. Both sides of the brain are activated, no matter what task you put to them. What is important in developing our skills as creative public relations practitioners is not so much where specific thinking skills are located in the brain but the fact that at least two specific modes of thought can be identified.

Convergent thinking, the so-called left-sided thinking, is the intellectual ability to logically evaluate, criticize and choose the best idea from a selection of ideas. Divergent thinking, the apparent right-sided thinking, is the ability of the intellect to think of many original, diverse and elaborate ideas. These contrasting thinking approaches are embodied in the two lead characters in the science fiction television classic, *Star Trek*. Mr Spock was the cool, analytical character, where everything was rationally observed and logically thought through; Captain Kirk, in contrast, was seen to employ more emotional, intuitive thinking, and being inspirational in his tackling of problems.

Green Light/Red Light thinking

A better way of looking at creative thinking than left/right brain is Green Light/Red Light thinking, with its stronger visual cues. For Green Light thinking, the colour, like that in a traffic light, is useful for symbolizing that anything can go, where the accent is on positively encouraging as many ideas as possible, whatever their status or validity. This equates with Captain Kirk (or what has been called right-hand brain thinking). Red Light thinking is sober analysis of what will or will not work, the rational judgement of an idea, equivalent to Mr Spock (and left-hand brain thinking). It is the 'Stop' sign for any idea that appears ludicrous or far-fetched – the rational mode of thinking for evaluating the relative merits of a proposal. Table 2.1 highlights the different characteristics of these two modes of thinking.

By having a clear understanding of the distinction between the two types of thinking, a practitioner can make far more productive use of time, and employ techniques to greater effect, generating more and varied creative ideas that offer added value.

Table 2.1 *Green Light and Red Light thinking*

Green Light thinking	Red Light thinking
Anything goes and is permissible	Analysis
Anything is possible	Judgement
The big picture is the context	Practicalities
Combinations of new elements	Functionality – will it work?
Positive impact of risk	Negative impact of risk
Looking at pictures, sound and movement	Details
Emotional and intuitive	Logical
Anything can happen in the future	Examine what worked in the past

Chapters 4–6 and 8 on creative ideas, brainstorming, and evaluation, examine in detail the skills of using Green Light and Red Light thinking.

 Look back on when you have previously tried to come up with a new idea. Try to recall how you used the different thinking modes of Green and Red Light thinking. Did you clearly separate their use? Did this have any effect on how ideas were actually generated?

THE MYTH OF 'LATERAL THINKING EQUALS CREATIVITY'

Mention the subject of creativity, or the task of coming up with ideas, and many people think of 'lateral thinking' as the route to being creative. It has almost become a generic description for a different way of looking at a problem: 'What we need is some lateral thinking on this'. While it is an important element, it is essential that practitioners should understand its proper meaning, role and context in creativity.

Convergent thinking believes that the mind's natural processes are ordered and logical; creativity, in contrast, is haphazard and illogical. It considers rationality and creativity to be different mental processes that are generally in conflict. Most problems are not new – the challenge is to view the problem in a new way.

The Concise Oxford Dictionary defines lateral thinking as: 'Seeking to solve problems by unorthodox or apparently illogical methods'. It was a concept defined by Edward de Bono in his book, *The Use of Lateral Thinking* (de Bono, 1990). In essence there are two modes of thinking, he says: the vertical mode and the lateral mode (identified in the previous section as Red and Green Light thinking).

Vertical thinking looks for what is right. It maintains that one thing must follow directly from another, concentrates on relevance and moves in the most likely direction. Lateral thinking changes: it looks for what is different, makes deliberate jumps, welcomes chance intrusions and explores the least likely possibilities. This may best be explained by the analogy of digging holes looking for treasure: vertical thinking makes a hole bigger, while lateral thinking leads you to dig a series of new holes in different locations.

Lateral thinking is about moving sideways when working on a problem, by trying different perceptions, different concepts and different points of entry. The term 'lateral thinking' can be used in two ways: as a specific set of systematic techniques used for changing concepts or perceptions, and for generating new ones; or it can be defined as exploring multiple possibilities and options instead of pursuing a single approach.

In the analogy of our buried treasure, if you had an accurate map showing its precise location then the obvious strategy is to dig vertically. However, if there are few sources of reference to guide you, then a strategy of many holes in different locations may yield the treasure you seek.

Lateral thinking is not the same as, or the sum of, creative thinking. It harnesses techniques that can be used in order to come up with a new idea. Although some writers take de Bono to task, arguing that his concept is in fact centuries old, he at least deserves credit in the way he has helped to popularize and promote the use of creative thinking techniques. Where lateral thinking and creative thinking part company is that true creativity is not the process of thinking of, for example, a hundred uses of a brick. Rather, it uses both Green and Red Light thinking to solve new problems by creating and acting upon ideas that offer added value to a task.

SUMMARY

1. Creativity is an incremental process – the instant Big Idea does not exist.
2. Rather than there being a distinct left- or right-hand side of the brain controlling our pattern of thinking, the brain actually has two distinct thought modes: Green Light and Red Light thinking.
3. Lateral thinking is a useful tool for creativity, but it is not the sum of creativity.
4. In similar fashion to those we have dealt with in this chapter, some of the 'facts' stated in this book are likely, at some point in the future, to be debunked as myths.

KEY WORDS FOR YOUR CREATIVITY VOCABULARY

- Green Light thinking.
- Incremental thinking.
- Lateral thinking.
- Red Light thinking.
- Vertical thinking.

3

How you think in 'boxes'

Everyone on this planet has a duty to think.
From What's it trying to say?*, a song performed by the 1970s pop star Dean Friedman on the opening of the Wakefield Media Centre*

SAME BOX, SMALLER BOX AND BIGGER BOX THINKING

This section looks at the myth of 'outside-the-box' thinking.

'Creativity' is in many ways a misnomer for the subject of how we can think up and use new ideas to achieve more with less. A more accurate description is that we are engaged in flexible thinking. Flexible thinking skills are the essence of creative practice.

Try this simple test with a group of colleagues. Without conferring, write down the first five words each of you associate with the following words:

Pen Blue Cake

Compare how many of the words are exactly the same on different lists. If you have the same words check if they are in the same order, written in capitals or lower case, or if there are any other differences. Having done this exercise with hundreds of groups in my creativity sessions I have never had a team where three or four people have the same five words.

The reason you each use different words, even with apparently relatively simple concepts such as 'pen', 'blue', and 'cake' is because you perceive the world, every object within it, uniquely through a picture frame shaped by your values, beliefs, experiences and connections. This metaphorical picture frame is called by psychologists a 'frame'. It can also be called a 'paradigm'.

The word 'paradigm' tends to be used to describe a frame of reference shaping how you perceive the world. It is generally used for describing a general mind state. In the creativity context a narrower definition of the term 'paradigm' meaning 'the boundaries of a perception' can be used.

Paradigms are a fundamental tool enabling each of us to make sense of the complex world we live in. Paradigms act as a filter, a short cut to manage the complexity of information in the world around you.

A typical photograph can contain over a million individual pixels. But you do not take in each individual pixel. Instead, you decide the picture represents a shape familiar to your experience. There is a marvellous apocryphal story about the artist Picasso who, as legend has it, was recognized by a stranger on a train. During the journey the stranger remonstrated with Picasso, asking why he didn't make his paintings more life-like. The artist wanted to know what the man meant by 'life-like'. In response the man took out from his wallet a photograph of his wife to which Picasso responded by observing how flat and small she was. The stranger had created a paradigm of the small, flat, representational image of his wife defining what he perceived as 'life-like'.

Paradigms can limit your vision of the world around you, acting as invisible boundaries, prison cells, that define the boundaries of your thinking and define your available options when you seek to solve problems.

Paradigms have been described as picture frames. The picture frame is created by assumptions. The most powerful analytical

tool – indeed, one of the most powerful creativity tools at your disposal – is a simple question: 'What assumptions are we making here?' This may seem like basic common sense, but as the old adage goes: 'What is common is not often sensible, and what is sensible is not often common.'

By asking 'What assumptions are we making here?' – and extending this question to identify the assumptions being made by you, your colleagues, competitors, the marketplace – you can identify the different paradigms at work that are dictating how the situation is being perceived.

A popular thinking challenge is the 'nine dot' exercise. The challenge is to connect all nine dots in Figure 3.1 by using four straight lines without lifting your pen off of the paper. It can be a frustrating exercise. (Even if they have done it before, most people forget the regularly proffered solution given in Figure 3.2 on page 34.)

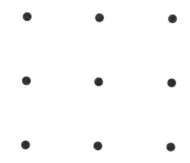

Figure 3.1 *The nine-dot problem*

This exercise is believed to have led to the phrase 'outside-the-box' thinking to describe a new way of doing, a solution outside the boundaries of how everyone else perceived it. I will go on to demonstrate how there is no such thing as 'outside-the-box' thinking. Before this it will be worth revisiting the nine dot challenge to explore even more potential solutions to emphasize how everyone's thinking is riddled with assumptions. Two solutions I have witnessed on my creativity courses which I have not come across in texts are as follows.

One delegate, a graphic designer, drew a four-line box around the nine dots, therefore connecting them all within the concept of a square; challenging the assumption about what we mean by 'connect' – does connecting have to involve a physical connection?

Another delegate drew four lines to connect the outer dots and then laid her pen down across the centre dots to connect all the dots; challenging the assumption that the lines had to be 'ink lines'.

It is possible to connect all the dots in three lines by drawing diagonal lines touching the outer edge of the top dot, the centre of the middle dot and the inner edge of the bottom dot and by repeating the journey successfully connecting all the dots; challenging the assumption that it is the centre of the dots that have to be connected.

You can even connect all nine dots in one line – by using a very large pen; challenging the assumption that the lines are of a smaller size to the dots.

It is possible to complete the exercise with no lines: by manipulating the surface, which is assumed to be paper, you can keep your pen still and bring the dots to the pen; challenging the assumption the surface is a flat, undynamic entity.

WHY THERE IS NO SUCH THING AS 'OUTSIDE-THE-BOX' THINKING

There is no such thing as 'outside-the-box' thinking. All thinking exists in a box. Certainly, 'outside-a-box' thinking exists. By thinking in a bigger dimension to any initial brief you are creating a bigger box. Your new thinking may extend or destroy the boundaries of the original paradigm, but all you have created is a bigger box, a new paradigm containing your new idea subsuming the original one. Your original idea will no doubt be subsumed by an even bigger box.

In your flexible, creative thinking you have three strategies:

- *Same Box thinking* – operating within the existing paradigms, where your message and content is within the confines of existing communication;
- *Smaller Box thinking* – changing an element or niche, or focusing on one smaller part of the existing paradigm;
- *Bigger Box thinking* – breaking down and going beyond the boundaries of the original paradigm to provide messages and content on a bigger scale.

EXAMPLES OF BIGGER BOX THINKING

A much-cited story about creative thinking is the one about the space race in the 1960s when the Americans spent the equivalent of £1 million and a year in research to get an ink pen to work in outer space and overcome the problems of low gravity. The Russians used pencils. The Americans had a paradigm of: 'How do we get a writing implement to work in outer space?' The Russians had a far bigger paradigm of: 'How do we get a writing implement to work in outer space?' By using a bigger box they opened up more options and alternatives for solving their problem.

The Beatles drummer Ringo Starr was once faced with a difficult question at the height of their fame in the mid-1960s: 'Are you a Mod or a Rocker?' Whatever answer he gave would alienate large sections of their fan base. His answer was: 'Neither, I'm a Mocker.' He astutely sidestepped the issue by refusing to answer the question solely within the two paradigms of 'Mod' or 'Rocker' given to him by the journalist. Instead, he created a bigger new paradigm of a whimsical concept of a 'Mocker'. (This was quoted in the 1964 film *A Hard Day's Night*.)

The challenges you face in devising Bigger Box thinking solutions are as follows:

- It is likely that if you are creating something new, you need an infrastructure to make it happen. This challenge is summed up by the joke about the person who invented the telephone: Who did the person ring? If you are doing something new, you will often need supporting mechanisms to make it happen.
- Existing interests may be undermined by any major paradigm changes and could put significant obstacles in the way of a potentially successful Bigger Box solution.
- The paradox of new alternatives in a pressure situation; the anxieties created by the need to come up with a quick response can be inimical to considering new and different alternatives. As a result, people will fall back on the known, the tried and tested rather than quickly explore Bigger Box alternatives, which could generate a radical, new way of doing and provide the optimum added-value answer. The greater the pressure and need for a different way of doing may often work against the likelihood for generating the best answer.

 Can you think of any examples in your work of where Bigger Box solutions have been tried? What obstacles did they have to overcome?

EXAMPLES OF SMALLER BOX THINKING

A more productive thinking strategy, certainly in the short to medium term is Smaller Box thinking, where you change just one aspect within the existing situation to achieve added value. It may be identifying a niche audience in your communications, changing the colour of your leaflet or logo, a different personality or action in a photocall.

Smaller Box thinking can work to inject quick wins and new life into an established campaign. Operating within established practice it can be easier to implement and may not require significant additional resource.

Some examples of Smaller Box thinking to generate creative added value are shown in Table 3.1.

Table 3.1 *Using Smaller Box thinking to generate creative added value*

Item	Smaller Box thinking
Audience	Target a niche group, or individuals within your already identified audiences
Timing	Change the timing of an existing activity
Print item	Change the colour, size, or shape
Brand	Create a sub-brand
Channel	Identify a more specific way of reaching your audience through an existing communications channel (for example using an advertising insert in a publication you are already using for media relations purposes)
Metaphor	Change or introduce a new metaphor in your communications

 Can you think of any examples in your work of where Smaller Box solutions have been tried? What obstacles did they have to overcome?

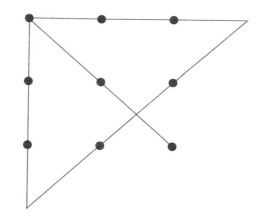

Figure 3.2 *Solution to the nine-dot problem*

BEING FLEXIBLE IN THE DIFFERENT BOXES YOU USE

By understanding that paradigms exist, you have a flexibility in recognizing and manipulating them. In addition, understanding that you have three different thinking strategies puts you at a competitive advantage over those limited to Same Box thinking. By posing the question: 'What assumptions are being made?' you can quickly dissect the paradigms shaping the thinking of others.

By adopting a helicopter view, above and beyond the situation, the creative thinker has the ability to jump outside the boxes limiting other people's perceptions. The flexible thinker can also reflect on and manipulate the relationship with boxes to achieve added value.

The challenge for successful creative thinking is to adopt flexible thinking to manage paradigms, so as not to be bound or constrained by what may hold others back. By effective redefining, either on a meta level, or changing a mindset to a minor adjustment, you can leverage significant communication advantage. Below are examples of how flexible use of paradigms delivered great added value in communications.

When faced with a challenge do not meet it head on, but use Bigger Box thinking or Smaller Box thinking to gain new perspectives.

Each of us sees the world uniquely. We also have a preferred thinking style in the way we perceive situations and the world around us. There are many different personality profiling methodologies to identify common characteristics of different types of thinking. It is as if we use a pair of spectacles to enable us to identify a situation before us and make sense of the different elements within our field of vision.

YOUR 'CREATIVE THINKING SPECTACLES'

I have created the idea of 'creative thinking spectacles' to provide a model that identifies and categorizes four common styles of thinking that govern how we manage any new situation and perceive the range and complexity of information contained within it.

There is no right or wrong type of 'creative thinking spectacles'. Each has its own advantages and disadvantages when it comes to generating and delivering ideas into action.

The four types of 'creative thinking spectacles', shown in Figure 3.3, are described below.

'Directors'

'Directors' have an extremely clear focus and are able to quickly delineate what they perceive as the 'problem'. Any 'problem' is seen in crystal clarity. 'Directors' have the advantage of being able to move quickly and decisively in dealing with their 'problem'.

Their limitations are that they may be too narrowly focused, perceiving only one or a few issues within a field of vision where, invariably, there will actually be many different options and a wealth of complexity. They may be blind to other opportunities, beyond their range of focus, which could have yielded far greater added value.

'Analysts'

'Analysts' see order and structure in the world around them. If it is not there they will do their best to create and impose a system and

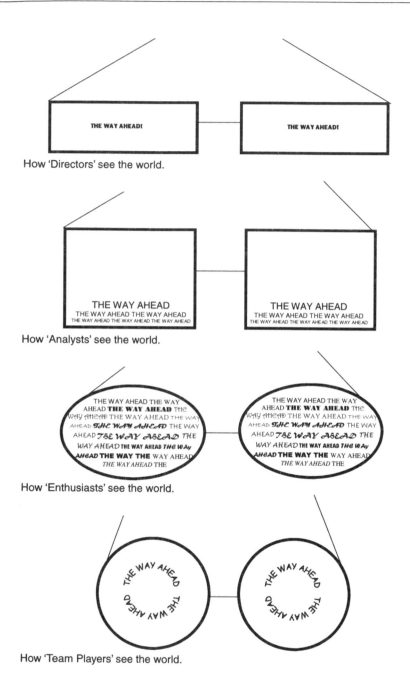

How 'Directors' see the world.

How 'Analysts' see the world.

How 'Enthusiasts' see the world.

How 'Team Players' see the world.

Figure 3.3 *Which glasses do you use?*

process on their world. They view the world as drawing options from a set range, and believe that through logic, analysis and deduction a solution will emerge.

Their limitations are that they will feel uncomfortable 'bathing in chaos' and need to move quickly to impose order on a situation. The process can also take over as the end goal, rather than the quest for added value to their context. They need to take multiple steps to progress to their goal, which may hinder rapid progress or even lead to paralysis by analysis.

'Enthusiasts'

As their name implies, 'Enthusiasts' have high levels of energy giving them far greater scope and vision than other people. They have a panoramic view of the world containing infinite variety and complexity. Not for them a situation consisting of 'a problem'; they can identify many other issues, in a rich variety of colours, tones and types. Their images can also contain a playfulness, contorting, combining or adapting the different elements before them.

By seeing a world of rich variety, they may however overlook the obvious, the clear-cut, which could offer added value. To their colleagues 'Enthusiasts' may appear to over-elaborate, not do the simple and obvious, because through their spectacles they see a different world which is not so simple or obvious but made up of rich diversity.

'Team Players'

As their name implies, 'Team Players' are team focused. They see a world dominated with its emotional undercurrents, where people are interconnected with an underlying network of personal relationships. They have vision tempered with a sensitivity of how people are feeling, and how they feel about a situation. When tackling a 'problem' they can avoid treading on people's toes or hurting feelings.

'Team Players' may be limited by placing too much emphasis on the emotional dimension to a situation, and the interconnectedness of the relationships within it, and consequently shy away from taking action to solve a 'problem'.

 Which 'creative thinking spectacles' category best describes you? What are the 'thinking spectacles' of your colleagues or decision makers who can approve or reject your creative ideas? (Chapter 4 has more details on how to use your knowledge of different thinking styles to sell your creativity.)

USING 'CREATIVE THINKING SPECTACLES' TO PROGRESS YOUR CREATIVE IDEA

A knowledge of these different thinking styles can also help you be more tolerant and understanding of working with colleagues in developing ideas. The directors, for example, who want quick, clear-cut answers can often be frustrated with their enthusiast colleagues who may elaborate many different alternatives. The challenge is to recognize and respect the different profiles and identify the optimum time and context to use them.

QUESTIONS ARE A CREATIVE PRACTITIONER'S BEST FRIEND

When faced with new situations there is a tendency to immediately think of new ideas. Certainly, if you have a number of ideas already at hand do capture them and make a brief note.

The crucial step is to ask a series of questions. Andy Gilbert of Go MAD research and consulting group uses a framework for thinking for whenever you want to make a difference to a situation. His checklist questions include:

- What are your reasons why? (Why is this important to me?)
- What goals are we defining?
- What are our priorities? (What possibility thinking do we need to use? What is most important? What do we need to do to plan in time?)
- What is our level of self-belief for success in this task? (Can it be boosted and improved?)
- What personal responsibility am I prepared to take?
- How can I involve others? (What are the key tasks to get others involved?)
- What do I need to do to take action?

The key quality of the creative person is to pose beautiful questions. As the German philosopher Arthur Schopenhauer observed: 'Talent hits a target no one else can hit; Genius hits a target no one else can see.' (Quoted on www.thinkexist.com.)

By posing questions you can help to identify the many assumptions you and everyone else are making and enable you to frame the challenge in new and original ways in your quest to be an outstanding creative communicator.

SUMMARY

1. You see the world within a picture frame, defined by your knowledge, experiences, values and beliefs. This picture frame can be called a 'paradigm'.
2. The flexible thinker has the ability to quickly analyse situations using Smaller Box thinking and Bigger Box thinking.
3. Each of us has a preferred way of viewing the world. By understanding the different types of 'spectacles' people use you can understand how they view the world differently.
4. Questions are the fundamental first step in generating ideas.
5. The better you define your questions, the more chance you are likely to deliver a creative solution.

KEY WORDS FOR YOUR CREATIVITY VOCABULARY

- Paradigm.
- Same Box, Smaller Box, Bigger Box thinking.

4

The creative process

THE FIVE 'I's

Contrary to the popular perception of creativity being a will-o'-the-wisp type of activity, the creative process can be divided into a number of distinct stages. In some instances it will be possible to trace the inception and development of an idea through each of these stages; on other occasions an idea may consciously appear to develop simultaneously through all the stages at once.

It was only about 400 years ago that scientists discovered that our brain, not our heart, was responsible for our intellectual activity. Real advances on how we go about being creative were not really significantly investigated until the early part of the 20th century. The physiologist Helmholtz and the mathematician Poincaré were first to divide the creative process into different phases.

Joseph Wallas, back in 1926, believed the creative process had four phases: a preparatory stage, followed by incubation, illumination and, lastly, verification. Joseph Rossman in the 1930s saw seven stages:

1. observation of need or difficulty;

2. analysis of need;
3. survey of all available information;
4. a formulation of all objective solutions;
5. a critical analysis of these solutions for their advantages and disadvantages;
6. the birth of a new idea – the invention;
7. experimentation to test out the most promising solution and the selection and perfection of the final embodiment by some or all of the previous steps.

Alex Osborn, who in the 1950s was one of the great pioneers of applying creative techniques for commercial use in advertising and marketing, also divided up the creative process, as follows:

1. orientation: pointing out the problem;
2. preparation: gathering pertinent data;
3. analysis: breaking down the relevant material;
4. ideation: piling up alternatives by way of ideas;
5. incubation: letting up to invite illumination;
6. synthesis: putting the pieces together;
7. evaluation: judging the resulting ideas.

More recently, Professor Morris Stein established a three-stage model:

1. hypothesis formation;
2. hypothesis testing;
3. communication of results.

The reason for outlining these different models of the creative process is to establish the credibility and substance of the concept. By recognizing that there is method in the creative process, practitioners can improve their effectiveness and identify any weaknesses in the chain – which can then be remedied.

It is also possible to highlight the common themes running through them all. Each includes a vital first step of identifying the problem, accompanied by the need to gather information. Most include a reference to what is called 'incubation', which will be described shortly. Then comes the actual stage of the idea being born, with the last stage characterized by some form of evaluation and implementation of the idea.

To help public relations practitioners have an effective, comprehensive and memorable model to use in understanding and harnessing the creative process, I have devised a mnemonic – the five 'I's of the creative process, which are:

1. Information.
2. Incubation.
3. Illumination.
4. Integration.
5. Illustration.

We shall consider each of these in greater detail below.

 Commit these five 'I's to your long-term memory. One trick for doing this is to use what are called 'trigger fingers'. Hold up your left hand. Touch your thumb with your other hand and say aloud 'Information'. With the next finger say 'Incubation', and continue along your left hand until you have gone through all the five 'I's.

INFORMATION

You cannot expect to build a cathedral with just two bricks of Lego.
A lesson to be learnt by us all

There are two elements to this first stage of the creative process of information: one is gathering the relevant information to assist with the task in hand. The second is posing the right questions.

Gathering the relevant information

The great advertising guru David Ogilvy describes in his book *Advertising* (Ogilvy, 1987) how he went about producing great ads: 'You don't stand a tinker's chance of producing successful advertising unless you start doing your homework. I have always found this extremely tedious but there is no substitute for it.' The first task in the creative process is to stuff your conscious mind with information and then to unhook your rational process. Your unconscious has to be well informed or your ideas will be irrelevant.

From my own experience as well as from talking to leading creative practitioners it seems (and this may upset some in the industry) that most ideas presented at pitches suffer from being irrelevant, unworkable, or outside the client's value system. Most creative ideas are, frankly, of poor quality – even from those who are regarded as creative. They very rarely end up seeing the light of day.

Despite the best efforts and intentions in climbing up the learning curve, you will find most of your ideas lack the relevant experience and knowledge to be truly effective. I find that I generally come up with genuinely outstanding ideas, which will work for the client, at least three to four months after working on an account.

 If you have written a creative proposal for a new client, or for an unfamiliar area of activity, look back at your earlier work and check if any of the ideas were subsequently carried out precisely as presented. It is most unlikely that they were.

There is also a need to obtain as much information as possible from the production 'coalface'. The American marketing guru Guy Kawasaki draws up in his book *How to Drive Your Competition Crazy* (Kawasaki, 1995) an amusing sequence of how research can be transformed within an organization and cause the original information to be significantly distorted. This sequence is shown in Table 4.1.

Table 4.1 *How information can be transformed*

Person	Viewpoint
Customer	It is a crock of shit, and it stinks.
Researcher	It is a container of faeces, and most unpleasant in smell.
Manager	It is an earthenware vessel of excrement, and it is very strong.
Director	It is a vase of fertilizer, and no one can resist its strength.
Vice-president	It contains substances that aid plant growth, and it is very potent.
Chief operating officer	It promotes growth, and it is very robust.
President	Let's implement this terrific idea because it will promote growth.

Furthermore, Regis McKenna in his book *Relationship Marketing* (McKenna, 1991) describes how, when researching for a client who made calculators, he watched a sales counter and observed people buying calculators. He noticed that people were weighing them in their hands and seemingly deciding that the heavier ones must somehow have more in them. His advice to the client was to add some technically unnecessary weight to their products – an insight not gained from reams of reports or expensive group interview panels but from simply hanging around a sales counter for half an hour.

The humorist P J O'Rourke describes how he accompanied a US government delegation to South America and observed how the 'experts' carried piles of dossiers on the country they were visiting. He, however, chose not to read the reports, but instead opted for a more pleasurable route by checking out a number of bars, speaking to the barmen and asking them about the current state of affairs. His verdict: he reckoned he obtained a far more accurate insight into the country than the so-called experts. He also got very drunk.

On training courses, I pose the question: 'How many people read the catalogues of ideas for public relations people, which are produced each day and contain pages of new opportunities, events and angles to use in your own work?' Usually, I am faced with a blank response. I then reframe the question: 'How many people read the newspapers every day?'

From my surveys of public relations practitioners, the majority will read maybe one or two newspapers a day, some may read two or three, and about one in five will read four or more, as well as magazines. Most outstanding creative practitioners read four or more newspapers a day; Gordon Forbes of consultancy Ptarmigan reads every national quality and tabloid before setting off for the office.

Most people say they do not have time to do this. Later in this book you will learn the skill of reading broadsheet newspapers such as the *Financial Times* in less than two minutes. Reading newspapers is an extremely important part of my working day, and it cannot be over-stressed how important this task is if you want to be a successful public relations practitioner. How, for example, in media relations can you know what type of story the *Financial Times* is interested in if you do not read it?

The information-gathering stage is fundamental to the success

or failure of the subsequent creative activities. Hence the analogy in this section's opening quote of using Lego bricks: the more bricks you have, the greater the potential to create new and different things.

Posing the right questions

The better we analyse first, the better we can synthesize later. The more intelligently we have picked our problems to pieces, the more likely we are to find the pieces that can be combined into the ideas that can lead to solutions. A vital part of the information stage is to provide a clear focus for the creative process to work upon. The old adage, 'A problem well stated is a problem half solved' is particularly apt. Also, raising the right question at the right time is another key skill of the creative practitioner.

Any able practitioner knows about the 'five Ws and an H' – What? Where? When? Why? Who? and How? – to include in a press release intro, yet such a practitioner often fails to pose the very same questions when receiving a brief for a task. So, the first task in gathering information is simply to get the answers to these six universal questions.

From experience, the problems cited by a client in giving a brief rarely reflect the true problem. How can you get to the root of an issue or find out if there are any hidden agendas? A simple technique is to ask 'Why?' at least five times.

Here is a real-life example. The brief from a prospective client was to raise its media profile in certain regional business press. My initial judgement was that this was a marginal requirement for what was judged to be their real marketing needs.

First 'Why' question: 'Why is the regional business media important?'
Client: 'Well, it's important to be seen in this medium.'
Second 'Why' question: 'Why is it important to be seen in this medium?'
Client: 'Well, some of our competitors have had some good coverage in this medium.'
Third 'Why' question: 'Why it is important to you that some of your competitors have got coverage in this sector?'
Client: 'Well, actually one of our senior directors recently left to set up on her own and got a big article about her new company in this media sector.'

Fourth 'Why' question: 'Why is that important to you?'
Client: 'Because our Chairman took it rather personally about this director leaving.'
Fifth 'Why' question: 'Why is that important in terms of your future public relations activities?'
Client: 'He's now getting on my back to ask why we haven't got any coverage like that.'

By persisting with the 'Why?' questions, it is possible to get to the root cause of the brief. The client in this particular instance was not after a comprehensive public relations strategy with a coherent media relations programme at all; he was just after what I call 'vanity ink' to settle a personal score.

When faced with a task, always restate the problem in as many ways as you can. Change the wording, take different viewpoints, try it in graphic form. Describe the problem to laypeople and also to experts in different fields. Says Graham Lancaster of Biss Lancaster:

> A good creative director of an advertising agency will expect a very full brief before putting their mind to a solution. They will want to immerse themselves in the client's history, in its production processes, quality control procedures, in its corporate style, in the way customers look at the market – all these and more before outline creative treatments are drawn up. Once the real creative brief has been thoroughly understood, an acceptable creative solution could become obvious to anyone. The skill is arriving at that very tight brief.

The problem will dictate the solution. The most profound tool when being creative is to challenge the assumptions that you have made about a problem. A useful device is a variation on the 'five Whys' technique, in which you ask, 'What am I assuming here?', and then pose and repeat the same question to the answer, then repeat the process again and so on.

By doing this, you are essentially helping to define the paradigm you face. In the context of creativity, a paradigm can be defined as the way we see the world – the 'frame' we put around our 'picture of the world'. This framing determines how our minds look at something and for the way we subsequently act. Paradigms determine our initial responses and generate our first ideas. They are characterized by the usual, easy way of doing and thinking,

guiding our decision making and providing a structure for the information and values we hold.

Whenever new situations are being faced, there is a tendency to impose invisible frameworks around the problem and to make assumptions. These false constraints can hamper our efforts in trying to come up with a creative solution.

The solution to this problem, and potentially to any task, is to think 'outside the box' and consider whether there are solutions you have missed because you have unconsciously imposed assumptions, constraints or rules. The map, as they say, is not necessarily the territory.

As quoted in Chapter 3, one of the best examples of an outside-the-box solution is the response given by Ringo Starr, when the Beatles were at the height of their fame in the mid-1960s and he was asked by an interviewer: 'Are you a Mod or a Rocker?' Ringo's response was quite brilliant: 'Neither, I'm a Mocker.'

Another example was a response given to the *Yorkshire Evening Press* during my time as a press officer for the pre-privatized Yorkshire Water Authority in the mid-1980s. The York-based news-paper was running a campaign against the Authority holding its board meetings in private. When Margaret Thatcher, then Prime Minister, visited the region, the newspaper took the opportunity in an interview to press her on this issue. Her response was that this was entirely in order, as the Authority did not determine policy. However, the newspaper quickly contacted an individual board member and asked if the board determined policy at its meetings, to which he replied that it did. Only then did the paper come on to the Authority and pose the question: 'Mrs Thatcher says the Authority does not determine policy at its board meetings but your board member says you do. Which one is right?'

This at first glance appeared to be an impossible quandary. Being a publicly funded body, it would risk a major political row if we were to say the Prime Minister of the land was wrong; equally, it could not very well say that its board member does not know what he is talking about. Our solution could have been lifted from the television programme *Yes, Minister*. Rather than contradict either view, we contrived a response that agreed with both of them! We said: 'They are both right. Parliament lays down the policy within which we operate and makes executive decisions. Within this context, the board makes policy decisions.' On one level this was complete gobbledegook, but by not being drawn

into the journalist's definitions of the options available, we succeeded in avoiding a major political row – as well as not alienating the board member.

Paradigms can range from assumptions based on incorrect information to deeply held mindsets that provide a strict order, determining how we see, what we do and how we operate in the world.

Paradigms are powerful things. If you learn how to recognize, challenge and, if necessary, destroy them, you can create new paradigms and thereby create added value. It is worth repeating that perhaps the most creative tool at your disposal is the simple question: 'What assumptions are we making here?'

INCUBATION

I work all the time, even in my sleep.

A sad confession

Craft shops often sell an attractive gift made by Guatemalan Indians. It consists of a small box containing six miniature dolls. Legend has it that before you go to bed at night you should tell each of the dolls a worry. When you wake up in the morning you go to the box and ask each of the dolls: 'Have you a solution to my problem?' Evidently, a solution to your problem then comes to mind.

One of the greatest 20th-century philosophers, Bertrand Russell, recalls how he would tackle problems:

Having by a time of very intense concentration planted the problem in my subconscious, it would germinate underground until, suddenly, the solution emerges with blinding clarity, so that it only remained to write down what had happened, as if in a revelation.

The South African folk singer Manadala Kunene Zulu evocatively describes his songwriting process in a *Sunday Times* article: 'I climb into bed. I lie there listening to the wind in the trees. Sometimes I hear my neighbour's dog barking. Then my eyes close and I wait for my songs to come.'

The Guatemalan Indians, Bertrand Russell and Manadala Kunene Zulu were describing the incubation stage of the creative process. Incubation occurs when the individual sets the problem aside for a while and does something else that is unrelated to it.

Poincaré, one of the originators of identifying this stage in the creative process, defines incubation as 'simply the facilitation of problem-solving by the passage of time'. A more modern-day example is Alan Preece of the University of East Anglia, who reflects: 'Sometimes, I try to solve a problem by not trying to solve it.' This approach is not one of being indifferent to the creative task. Rather, by putting the idea on the back burner you are allowing at least three positive things to take place. First, you are putting the problem into perspective. Second, by planting a seed in your mind you are like the biological analogy, allowing it to develop within your subconscious. Third, when you return to consider an idea or problem, you will probably approach it with a different set of assumptions.

Incubation is essentially harnessing your subconscious mind to help in problem solving. There is considerable evidence that some of the greatest thinkers were great relaxers: Einstein was a daydreamer (he had an undemanding job in the Swiss Patent Office) and spent much of his leisure time sailing on a lake. Knowing when to turn away from a problem and leave it for a while, for the incubation process to work, is an essential skill. It takes confidence, good planning, and a belief in your own abilities to let ideas saunter in at their own pace.

Incubation works not only at a deep subconscious level, but also during what is commonly referred to as 'daydreaming'. Many great thinkers have often been described by contemporaries as 'absent minded' when their minds are seemingly miles away from the immediate task at hand. From experience, I would suggest that what is described in such cases is actually a creative person actively working on a task, albeit through strong mental imagery rather than a conscious form in their immediate environment. A friend of mine once described this state as not absent minded, but 'present minded, elsewhere'.

Most people fail to manage this incubation phase effectively. How often, when presented with a report that is going to be the subject of a brainstorming session or that is requiring your input in some way, do you read it at the last minute (or even at the meeting)? Yet by recognizing the existence of the incubation phase, reading such information should be one of the first things you do, rather than the last. As a result of entering the information into your mind, it is then possible to move completely away from it and

do something else. It allows the incubation process to digest and turn over the information in your subconscious.

As well as being a good tool for creativity, the incubation process is also useful in time management. When writing your daily list of 'Things to Do' (and maybe even a 'Things Not to Do' list), do it at the end of the day rather than first thing in the morning. By revisiting the list in the morning, further ideas will have emerged overnight as a result of incubation, and so you can highlight new tasks or emphasize different priorities.

Another tip is to use what can be called 'Penultimate Scheduling'. Most people tend to treat a forthcoming break, such as a weekend or a holiday, as the deadline for completing a task. They then feel good about getting something out of the way before the break. However, the break can act as a further incubation period, known as an 'Incubation Rest', and during this period further ideas can occur – although, unfortunately, the work may have already been submitted and so it will be too late to capitalize on any additional thoughts. Using Penultimate Scheduling, the ideal scenario is to complete the task before any break and then timetable the deadline so that it will accommodate any extra ideas created during the Incubation Rest.

So how does the subconscious work to allow incubation? Unfortunately, no one really knows. The inner mind is still largely unexplored. But although we may not know about the mechanics within the subconscious, by recognizing the process of inputting information and the later output of ideas, we can harness and manage the incubation stage to greater benefit, and so be more creative public relations practitioners.

ILLUMINATION

Imagine a business that received hundreds of phone calls each day from prospective customers, but only bothered to follow up a random few. Would that be good business management? That is the contempt with which we treat the many ideas we generate every day.

An observation on how we manage our own inspirations

The most famous example of illumination, which has since become the symbol of scientific discovery, is Archimedes' cry of '*Eureka!*'

when solving the problem for the King of Syracuse about how much gold was in the royal crown. Similar to the experience of Bertrand Russell with his description of a 'revelation' that provides a solution with blinding clarity, this great man experienced the 'illumination' stage of the creative process.

We have all experienced what seems like a 'flash of inspiration'. Most people make the assumption that such thoughts have come 'out of the blue'. In fact, these ideas are the rapid action of a process preceded by a period of information and incubation. Illumination then arises, and consists of seeing two previously unrelated items and making a link between them for the task in hand.

Most people fail to remember their dreams each night. They also fail to note all the creative illuminations they generate each day. How often does an original idea come to mind but we fail to note it down and it soon becomes forgotten, possibly for ever?

Ideas are thoughts, and thoughts are fleeting. Unless you make the effort to document your ideas, you will lose many of them. There is absolutely no way to predict when a great idea is likely to pop into your mind. The only way to reduce the risk of losing it is to be prepared at all times. The act of writing or recording the illumination also impresses the idea more deeply in your mind for further incremental creativity to take place, and that process offers scope for further illumination.

There are habits and techniques to help you harness any illuminations you generate. The simple task of having pen and paper handy is an obvious solution. Ralph Waldo Emerson warned: 'Look sharply after your thoughts. They come unlooked-for, like a new bird seen in your trees and, if you turn to your usual task, disappear.' There is the great rock 'n' roll story of the Rolling Stones' guitarist Keith Richard, who slept with his guitar and a tape player. He got up one morning and rewound the tape, to hear the opening riff to *(I Can't Get No) Satisfaction*, followed by 30 minutes of him snoring. Luckily, Keith recognized the need to capture and keep a record of his illuminations and provided a classic song for ageing hippies everywhere (and often the high point of public relations staff Christmas parties across the land).

It is possible to hunt for inspiration and illumination. The writer Joseph Conrad habitually took a bath for spells of illumination, while the composer Brahms claimed his best musical flashes while shining his shoes. Table 4.2 lists some other situations for getting

good ideas, taken from among those in the public relations industry.

All of those listed are in fact capitalizing upon what is called 'low cortical awareness', where the front-of-brain consciousness seems to step down a gear while doing a relatively menial task. At work, whenever given a problem, I will try and describe it as soon as possible, in order to provide a kind of brief to myself. I can then let my subconscious work on it, even when consciously busy with other things. I also take advantage of occasions whenever doing any task not needing intense concentration – for example, swimming, circuit training, or decorating – where, at the outset, I brief myself on a problem and let my subconscious work on it. By the end of the task, more often than not, a series of illuminations will provide a solution.

Table 4.2 *A mini survey among public relations practitioners: Where do you get your best ideas?*

Practitioner	Ideas location
Mark Borkowski	In taxis
Paul Carroll	In the car
Max Clifford	While listening to boring people
Steve Gebbett	While doodling
Andy Green	In the shower
Alan Preece	While walking

Psychologists have identified what is called the 'alpha state', the period when you are either just falling asleep or just waking, as a route to reach the thoughts of the unconscious mind. It is believed that the 'critical censor', which normally stops your conscious mind accepting new ideas, shuts down. Certainly, when you are just stirring in the morning, try to capture as many of the thoughts you have as possible; if you don't, they will rapidly disappear. One trick is to go to bed early one night a week. The chances are that you will wake up earlier and have more time to recognize that you have had new thoughts or ideas and be able to make a note of them. Also, first thing on arriving at the office, instead of attacking the morning's post make a note of any illuminations that occurred overnight or on your way to work.

Here are some suggestions of different methods for capturing your ideas from a variety of sources (some being more practical than others!):

- a notepad;
- index cards;
- self-sticking notelets;
- a Dictaphone;
- a cassette recorder;
- mind maps (described in Chapter 5);
- a palmtop computer;
- a personal organizer;
- a perspex sheet and wax crayon for the shower or swimming pool;
- a personal assistant who follows you everywhere with a notepad!

Once you start to capture your illuminations, create an ideas bank to deposit your notes about them (such as a shoebox or a desk drawer). Another tip is to use a standard, distinctive, unique designation for indicating ideas, making them stand out clearly within any text, so that they can be found by a computer search (such as '!!This is an idea!!').

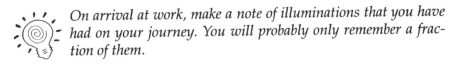 *On arrival at work, make a note of illuminations that you have had on your journey. You will probably only remember a fraction of them.*

INTEGRATION

Great musicals are not written, they are rewritten – the same goes for great PR campaigns.

Apologies to Stephen Sondheim

Imagine that I told you I had a great idea for a painting and it will consist of a portrait of a woman's head. Oh, and she will be smiling. Or suppose I said I had a brilliant idea for a book where the main character's father gets killed, and he thinks his mother may be involved and, oh yes, he later claims to see the ghost of his father. Are you likely to respond with raptures of: 'What brilliant

ideas they are!' No, but you may recognize them as the basis of two of the greatest works of creativity ever produced, namely Leonardo da Vinci's *Mona Lisa* and Shakespeare's *Hamlet*.

The creative qualities of both works of art rest not in their concept, but rather in the qualities of craft, structure, insight and wider resonance, as expressed in their particular medium. The Bard's work is admired not so much for the inspiration for an original story, but rather for the execution of his craft in its poetry, playwright skills and insight into the human mind and condition in relation to a timeless theme.

Pioneers of the study of creativity, such as Poincaré, refer to a creative process consisting of what this book calls the information and illumination steps. Poincaré then highlights a final verification stage, where the idea is checked out to see if it actually works. However, this understates the creative dimension at work in the application of any initial creative thoughts achieved through illuminations. Ideas are generated while the creator is working in the medium, in what can be called the integration stage of the creative process.

The brain does not follow passively through the implementation of the original idea or illumination, but may be constantly adding new elements, making refinements, or fundamentally redrafting the task. Consequently, any work is not just verifying an original idea, but is using the incremental nature of the creative process to develop possibly an entirely new creative product. Artists alter paintings and writers redraft material.

Take press releases. From your briefing (the information stage), you may rapidly go through the incubation stage where you have an idea (an illumination), before you actually write anything down. However, once you start writing you are likely to start adding extra elements. For example, a key 'trigger' word may come to mind and will be added. You might then think of a useful alliteration, or metaphor, to be used in a quote, and so on. While you are writing, a series of further ideas will emerge. The end result may be completely different from what you had originally envisaged.

When you are truly concentrating your thoughts and attention on performing a task, such as writing a press release, you are living and breathing within that medium. An analogy is an artist working on a picture. At the information, incubation and illumination stages, the artist may have in his mind's eye an image that he

intends to capture on canvas. The integration stage is a virtual world, of the artist actually living in the picture. While he is concentrating on working in the medium, in his mind he is inside the picture, and responding to its environment. In doing so, every movement, action, or change of direction alters how the picture will finally look.

By working in your particular medium, whether you are an artist or a public relations professional, you can provide added value through the execution of the idea in this integration stage.

 Look back on any recent creative work you may have produced. Analyse how many of the ideas contained within the end product you had before starting, and how many originated while working on the task.

ILLUSTRATION

The best ideas I have had are in the wastepaper basket.
And so says every outstanding creative public relations practitioner

There was once a man who offered to provide, for a large sum of money, an idea that would double the consumption of a new shampoo. More than that, the idea was a single word. But that single word would only be revealed on payment of his considerable fee. The company considered, and came to the conclusion that any idea that would actually double the consumption of shampoo would be well worth the money. Pocketing his cheque, the man stood before the board. 'My idea is as follows,' he said. 'You know the list of instructions on the side of the bottle? Well, add a word to the end. The word is... "repeat".'

I was faced with this example, featured in a travel magazine article, by a creativity course delegate after lecturing on the myth of the Big Idea. 'What about this example,' was the challenge: 'Is this not a Big Idea? A stunningly brilliant idea?' Certainly a good idea. But what if the idea had merely been recorded in a 240-page marketing report, and was one idea listed on page 197 subsection 12.2 among many other suggestions on 'How to improve the marketing of shampoo X'? What considerably enhanced the status of this idea was its presentation: the idea was initially hidden from view; its potential benefits were clearly spelt out; and only when

the audience was aroused to an intense state of curiosity and desire was it eventually unveiled. Rather like how a striptease artiste performs, the consultant in the story had tantalized, aroused interest, and finally offered what was promised.

What has this to do with creativity? The answer is that selling and presenting an idea is a critical stage. Don't believe that an idea will somehow sell itself. This stage of the creative process – the illustration stage – can be more important than the earlier stages of producing outstanding ideas.

Moving away from the world of marketing consultants and strippers, there are many notable examples of ideas failing to be recognized because they were not effectively sold. Who first put forward the theory of evolution by natural selection? 'Charles Darwin', most people would reply. Yet, Patrick Matthew, a Scottish botanical writer, actually did so 10 years before Darwin. Why had he gone unnoticed? Matthew's outstanding idea failed to get recognition as a result of his lowly position and because it also appeared at the end of a book on trees.

Clearly, how an idea is subsequently 'sold' is an important stage in the process that moves from creating an idea to its final implementation. From my own observations, most great ideas that ended up in the wastepaper basket did so because they were not effectively sold to the relevant decision makers to enable them to be progressed.

What can the public relations practitioner do to manage this stage of the creative process to maximum effect? There are a number of key elements that need to be identified and considered. They include:

- legitimizing the source of the idea;
- timing;
- translating the idea;
- keeping within brand values;
- presenting within the context of a relationship.

We shall look at these in turn below.

Legitimizing the source

Academic studies on how great creative ideas emerge identify a key stage in the creative process as that when the idea is accepted

by a key reference group. Following the production of a new work, others in the particular field consider and acknowledge the work as 'creative'. For example, in the world of art, a key role is played by gallery owners, or in science by other scientists. This involvement gives the new idea credibility and status, so that it is regarded as correct and valid. It then becomes part of the accepted culture, as a work of creativity.

In public relations, the source of an idea will often dictate how it is subsequently regarded. Whether you are a junior executive, part of an in-house department, or a member of a small consultancy, there will be occasions when you may feel annoyed that your particular idea has been rejected or not developed as you would wish. Yet exactly the same idea from a more senior member of staff, from a consultancy, or from a larger consultancy (respectively) will be given the go-ahead because it appears to have the validity of a more legitimate source.

This aspect of working life can be frustrating but the challenge, if you are in the situation, is to use your creative skills to let other people have your way. It is possible creatively to engineer a situation for the source of your original idea to appear to have been made by a senior manager within your organization, or by the client, or to have come from a respected outside source. By creatively transferring the ownership of the idea, you can overcome a key obstacle to its fruition.

Alternatively, it may be possible to organize the way in which an idea is created, so as to give it legitimacy and to overcome a potential obstacle. At one of our training courses, a delegate revealed a problem with a client who would constantly reject every idea the consultancy put forward. 'He would always say he was looking for the Big Idea and nothing he was proffered seemed to come up to this expectation,' was the cry from an increasingly frustrated practitioner. Even though (as explained earlier in this book) the Big Idea does not exist, the problem here, I felt, was that the client did not know what he wanted; the consultancy could have carried on unproductively, forever coming up with ideas and repeatedly getting knocked back.

The answer was to use what I call a 'Buy-in ownership' solution: involve the client in generating the initial idea by being part of the consultancy's brainstorming activities. Through this the client *de facto* legitimizes the process and makes it harder subsequently to denigrate or discard the ideas proposed.

Timing

The secret of great comedy is... timing. Equally, timing is an important skill in the illustration stage of selling creative ideas. If you present an idea to a decison maker when it is too embryonic and not fully developed, there may be a danger of its being killed off before birth.

Most people would suggest that the time to discuss an idea with others is after you have thought it through, weighed up its pros and cons, and anticipated any likely objections. There may, however, be occasions when you can involve the decision makers. Or you can adopt a strategy of showing a range of ideas at an early stage of their development in order to gain initial feedback and comment. Alternatively, you could consider fully developing a specific idea, perhaps with mock-ups of the proposed treatment and coverage.

In presenting ideas, a useful technique is 'the Agatha Christie' or 'the Slow Reveal'. This tactic was used in the example described earlier of the man who sold the idea of generating greater use of shampoo. The skill of presenting ideas is an area where public relations practitioners can learn from their colleagues working in advertising. When presenting an advertising campaign, a half-decent agency will not go into a meeting and say: 'Here are the ads, what do you think of them?' Rather, like the person with the shampoo idea, they will initially elaborate on the needs of the situation, and then highlight the potential benefits of the proposed solution(s). Only then will the client actually get to see the ad.

An alternative strategy is named after the television detective, 'the Colombo'. Here, the end solution is presented at the outset and the justification for the proposal is given afterwards.

Contrast these to the presentation style of the typical public relations practitioner. While there are many outstanding presenters, many are failing to do full justice to the quality of their creative work. Consequently, perfectly good ideas may never see the light of day and yet another great public relations campaign will look set to end up in the wastepaper basket.

Another facet of timing is never to present new ideas for consideration either first thing on a Monday morning or last thing on a Friday; lunchtimes should also be avoided. The target audience will either give insufficient time for consideration, or will be distracted by other matters.

Translating the idea

Perhaps the most common reason that great ideas fail to get approval is the failure to translate the exciting, brilliant, effective thought from the mind of the originator to those who have the power to sanction it. Far too often, creative people can get carried away with the vividness and coherence of the creative image in their *own* minds. They assume everyone else will see it in the same concrete detail and similarly recognize its potential. What is overlooked is the need to translate the image in the originator's mind into something understandable by a third party. The idea will not sell itself.

There are two fundamental approaches in the selling of an idea that most practitioners fail to address: the preferred thinking mode and the personality profile of the targeted decision maker.

Preferred thinking mode

Research into Neuro Linguistic Programming has shown that people have at least three preferred modes in the way they think, communicate and receive communications. By identifying a decision maker's preferred thinking mode, you can present your ideas in a format that is most likely to be understood, accepted and approved.

It is possible to identify someone's preferred thinking type by the language they use, and by their body language. The three categories of thinking mode are as follows:

1. *Visual thinking* is used by people whose thought process makes pictures in their minds. About 35 per cent of the population are in this category. They tend to use words such as 'Can you show it to me?', 'That's a bright idea', 'I can picture that', 'It's pretty clear to me' or 'Looks good to me'. When selling a creative idea to a visual-thinking person, paint pictures with your words – in particular, use appropriate metaphors, but also consider using visual props such as charts, diagrams, and copies of newspapers. When Manchester-based agency Communique presented its ideas when pitching for the Boddingtons brewery account, it used a video showing its staff in a pub – drinking Boddingtons, of course – with different staff members putting forward different ideas. This unusual approach gave greater status to their ideas and provided a distinct visual contrast to the other consultancies pitching for the account.

2. *Auditory thinking* is used by those who like to listen to the way you say things – the pitch, pace, timbre and intonation of your voice are important in the communication. These are an esti-mated 25 per cent of the population. Their language can be identified by phrases such as: 'That sounds good to me', 'Tell me what it can do', 'I don't like the sound of that', 'It has got a good ring to it' or 'I hear what you are saying'. When presenting your ideas to these people, emphasize the sound of what you are saying. Where possible, use more than one person to present the creative ideas to give variety to the sound of what is being said.

3. *Kinaesthetic thinking* accounts for the remaining 40 per cent of the population, and they get their information from touch, gut instincts, hunches, and may often get goose-pimples. Key words and phrases are: 'This feels good', 'I need to grasp the details', 'This touches me' and 'I can get a handle on this'. The introductory handshake is an important element of the meeting, along with opportunities to hold samples, or props, relating to your creative proposals.

Although computer-based presentation systems have led to greater use of visual props by public relations consultancies, most pitch proposals still tend to have an emphasis on talking heads. Consequently, there is an inherent emphasis on auditory communications, which is used primarily by only 25 per cent of the population.

In meetings, most practitioners use a proposal document that is given out at the end of the presentation – to avoid the decision maker reading ahead of the presenter. Yet this works against kinaesthetic thinkers, where feel and touch are important. You should accommodate them by providing handouts, perhaps featuring extracts from the proposal report, to give them some-thing relevant to touch and hold.

In presenting ideas, the more you can use the preferred thinking mode of the decision maker, the more readily you can present your creative idea to maximum effect. Public relations staff often bemoan decision makers who could not see the potential of an idea. On reflection, it may have been the case that the decision makers' lack of vision was because they were non-visual thinkers, and therefore would have difficulty visualizing any ideas. Had the ideas been presented to appeal to their auditory or kinaesthetic

modes of thinking, perhaps the creative ideas would have been approved.

Personality profile – an extension of your 'creative thinking spectacles'

Essentially, the human race is made up of billions of individuals, each a person and each unique. Yet it is possible to put the entire human race into a few small groups or profiles. This can be achieved by identifying a number of key types or profiles of people, with each having a preferred way of dealing with information and making decisions.

It is important to stress that there is no right or wrong profile group. Nor is it better to be in one group than any other. By understanding the personality profile of the key decision maker, you can present your creative idea to him or her in the style, flavour and format this is most likely to gain acceptance.

Figure 4.1 *Which symbol best represents you? Choose just one of these symbols to sum you up*

Although there are numerous personality profiling systems detailed in various texts, a useful system for public relations practitioners breaks down the human race into just four types (see Figure 4.1). A number of different descriptions have been used for each of these, including one that uses the key elements of an advertisement (headline, illustration, body copy and logo) to describe each group, and another that uses just symbols. The four profiles are as follows:

- 'Headline' types, or 'Directors', characterized by the symbol △, are strong on leadership and control their emotions. They are likely to be independent, energetic, assertive and lively. When presenting these people with ideas, you need to emphasize the

tangible benefits and results that will be achieved by your proposal. They do not want to be excited by the idea itself but by what it will achieve for them. As these people like to be in control and like making decisions, you should present them with a range of options so that they can choose, and feel they are making the selection of what they believe will be best. *How to spot*: Because they are very much action people, meetings and phone conversations tend to be brief and to the point. Their desks are very action-orientated and their offices may have evidence of achievements, such as award certificates, on the walls.

- *'Illustration' types* or *'Enthusiasts'*, characterized by the symbol ξ, are people who are also strong on leadership but who are willing to show their emotions. Such people can be thought of as competitive, dynamic, excitable and optimistic. They are likely to appreciate an idea for its own value rather than for its end result. When presenting to this type, because enthusiasts want recognition, you should emphasize personal thanks and fame that will result from using the idea, such as 'This is a potential award-winner.' Your creative idea needs to appear radical, different, innovative, dramatic and fun. *How to spot*: Often the life and soul of the party, they are very sociable but poor at remembering names. Desks may appear untidy and meetings often start late and may stray off the agenda. Hairstyle tends to be carefree and clothing may not be precisely coordinated.

- *'Logo' types* or *'Team Players'*, characterized by the symbol \bigcirc, are low in leadership skills but are high in showing emotions. They are likely to be polite, sensitive, accurate and realistic. They value consensus and tend not to enjoy making decisions. When presenting ideas to these people, you should emphasize support and be personally helpful. They need to feel included and be liked; 'Team Players' want acceptance. The seller needs to encourage democracy, to express equality, and to reduce the anxiety in having to make a decision. Options such as: 'See how this goes in the first instance' or 'Appoint us for a trial period only' will help lessen the anxiety that 'Team Players' feel in making a decision. *How to spot*: They will often spend the first part of a meeting talking about social things, their family or friends. They are good at remembering names. Desks may have photos of their children or pets. Hairstyles tend to be

slightly carefree and they tend to dress for their individual comfort.

- *'Body Copy' types, or 'Analysts,'* characterized by the symbol ▢, are low in leadership skills and also control their emotions. Such people are thoughtful, calm, reliable and steady. In presenting ideas to them, you need to provide details and explain the processes that went into how the idea was generated, along with an analysis of its implementation. This category wants details, and tends to be cautious and conservative. *How to spot*: They are very punctual, and they will prefer to have a set agenda. Desks and offices are very orderly and tidy. Usually crisper in clothes style and tend not to have a hair out of place.

By identifying the personality type of the decision maker, you can select the best way of presenting your ideas. When I worked in an advertising agency, there always used to be quandary about 'Do we show the client one ad or a selection?' Invariably, we would take pot luck and not always get it right. However, by having an understanding of personality profiling, we know what to do: if we are presenting to a 'Headline' style of client, we provide a range of options, as they like making decisions; 'Illustration' types similarly want a range of options as they enjoy dealing with different ideas and making their own input; however, a 'Body Copy' style of client will want to see a logical process culminating in one ad as the solution to their problem; and for 'Logo' types the challenge is to select one ad and state that 'we can run with this one if you like, but if it is not totally to your suiting we can be part of your team to readily come up with an alternative', thereby lessening any anxiety about making a decision and emphasizing a key value of being a team player.

What if you are presenting your creative ideas to a group of people of different personality profiles? The trick here is to identify the key decision maker, and suit the presentation of your creative ideas to that person's requirements. Use opportunities such as an open invitation to visit your premises or to take part in a social event to any 'Team Player' members of the client team, and leave a detailed proposal document with the 'Body Copy' member of the team.

Closely analyse the way you describe things and discover what is your preferred thinking mode. Try to identify the preferred thinking mode of a key decision maker who can sanction your creative ideas. Or what personality profile best describes you? Consider how you can apply these techniques in getting greater acceptance of your ideas.

Keeping within brand values

Effective creativity must not compromise the brand values of the organization or product. One reason for creative ideas being rejected is that the client or organization does not feel 'comfortable' with the proposal. Usually, there is a response of: 'This is not for us.' Yet often it is the individual manager being overprotective and overcautious – perhaps motivated by covering his or her back within the organization – rather than any real assessment of the organization's brand values.

To guard against this when presenting creative proposals, you can use a technique called 'the Inoculation Effect'. This works rather like the way a vaccine can inoculate, by harnessing the virus it is guarding against. By stating a potential negative to the creative idea at the outset of the presentation, such as: 'You might be concerned how this creative proposal will affect your image in...', you effectively inoculate the proposals against being evaluated negatively by the recipient. Beginning the communication with a negative, and providing an answer to it, may help overcome a potential objection that could have wrecked the chances of the proposals being considered. (In Chapter 10 there is further information on how to handle objections to creative ideas.)

Presenting within the context of a relationship

An effective presentation can only be achieved if, before delivering any formal reasoning of a case, there is an understanding of the target's perspective and frame of mind. Most people, when making presentations, go straight to the details of the merits of their case. They fail to prepare the ground in terms of truly understanding the motivations at work and the way new information will be perceived by the audience. Always take stock of the other person's perspective and experiences before delivering any hard sell of a creative idea.

By managing the elements and making use of the techniques described here, practitioners can seek to manage the illustration stage to ensure that their creative product can be brought to fruition, and avoid a potential fate in the wastepaper basket.

Look back to any occasion when what you thought were outstandingly creative ideas were rejected. How could you have sold these ideas better?

SUMMARY

1. Creativity has five stages: the five 'I's of Information, Incubation, Illumination, Integration and Illustration.
2. You should already have committed the names of the five 'I's of the creative process to your long-term memory.
3. By understanding the creative process and its distinct stages, you can identify any weaknesses in your efforts to produce a creative solution.
4. How you sell an idea can be more important than the quality of the idea itself.

KEY WORDS FOR YOUR CREATIVITY VOCABULARY

- Alpha state.
- Auditory thinkers.
- Body Copies.
- Five 'I's.
- Headlines.
- Illustrations.
- Inoculation effect.
- Kinaesthetic thinkers.
- Legitimizing the source.
- Logos.
- Paradigms.
- Translate the idea.
- Visual thinkers.

5

Green Light thinking: creative techniques

How do you come up with a creative idea when faced with a blank sheet of paper? Easy. Don't have a blank sheet of paper.

A tip

Every working day, public relations practitioners are faced with demands to come up with creative answers to problems. Often, the creative dimension will be overlooked and the first solution at hand will be used as the way ahead for a particular task. A fundamental message of this book is to seek, wherever possible, to provide *added value* from the creative process.

Outstanding practitioners may display what is called unconscious competence in appearing to be able to come up with ideas intuitively. Yet most of them employ the processes and techniques detailed in this book, albeit subconsciously. There is no magic wand for coming up with ideas, but there *are* a large number of techniques to help anyone be creative. These techniques, coupled with a knowledge and understanding of the creative process – with its five stages, named respectively, Information, Incubation, Illumination, Integration and Illustration – will help considerably to improve your creative abilities.

SUGGESTED TECHNIQUES FOR STIMULATING IDEAS

Rather than trying to learn every creative technique parrot-fashion that is being suggested here, try instead to understand the process behind the techniques. This will enable you to consider whether or not it is relevant for the task in hand, whether or not you feel comfortable with it, and – most importantly – whether or not it produces results.

And bear in mind that any technique to encourage creativity will aim to achieve one or more of the following. It should:

- suspend judgement or perspectives;
- stimulate a quantity of ideas;
- focus on the detail of a situation or problem;
- generate combinations of different elements;
- give a structure or discipline to your information gathering, idea creation and evaluation of a situation;
- encourage a creative state of mind;
- prevent you from being anxious;
- make time for you to be creative.

The last point may seem fairly obvious, but one of the common laments of public relations practitioners is just that: 'We don't have time to be creative.' Yet it is obvious that unless time is allowed for being creative, how can you harness your creative potential? George Bernard Shaw flippantly observed: 'Few people think more than two or three times a year. I've made an international reputation for myself by thinking once or twice a week.'

The techniques here will help your time management by providing a framework to generate ideas – sometimes in minutes, even in seconds – and without your being anxious about it. When using techniques, I tend to find that a 90:5:5 rule applies: 90 per cent of new ideas or permutations you will generate will be of poor quality (or worse!), 5 per cent will be ideas you would have thought of anyway, but 5 per cent will be ideas or permutations you would not initially have come up with.

The suggested techniques are set out next.

Establish the Creative Range

Whenever faced with a well-defined task, such as coming up with

an idea for a launch event or photocall, establish a Creative Range. Pose what is called 'the Safe Bet' question: 'What is the very least, the safest, most conservative idea we could use?' Then ask yourself a second question: 'What is the most outrageous idea we could have here to solve the problem?' so as to create the Extreme Option.

By posing these two questions, you have created the initial limiting parameters of the available creative options. This can be visualized as a line (see Figure 5.1) with, at one end, the Safe Bet Option and at the other end the Extreme Option, the space between providing the Creative Range of the situation. Then ask: 'What further ideas can I come up with here?' and go on to note all the ideas that come to mind. And to start with, just write down the first thought that comes to mind for the Extreme Option; while you think up further ideas, even more outrageous ideas may emerge.

By establishing the Creative Range, you are immediately taking the pressure off yourself in that, first, at the very least you have a safe option to fall back on, and second and more importantly, you are harnessing the incremental nature of the creative process. You are not looking for elusive Big Ideas, but rather small ideas to fit within the Creative Range. This also helps to suspend judgement because you are not automatically screening every idea but merely filling in the Creative Range.

Figure 5.1 *The Creative Range*

I once met a man who claimed to have written the copy for the Consulate menthol cigarette advert, which had a slogan, 'Cool as a mountain stream'. I asked him how he came to think of this idea. He replied: 'I just thought of what is the opposite of a horrible, smelly cigarette, and I came up with a vision of a mountain stream.' By establishing the Creative Range you are not only helping to provide a platform for your creative thought process, you may also generate an extreme idea, which in itself could provide the solution to the task.

Work backwards from the future

When faced with a task, rather than think: 'What do we need to do next?', simply visualize the end objective and work backwards from that point.

For example, it can often be frustrating when faced by a client or colleague who says: 'We have just spent several thousand pounds on a market research survey. Here are its findings – can you make any use of them?' When using a market research survey to generate editorial coverage (rather than as a tool for gaining marketing intelligence), consider news angles required for obtaining media interest. By working backwards through the process of producing a market research survey, you can draft the questions to engineer the type of data required to produce editorially interesting material. So try to have an input into the drafting of market research questionnaires. This is preferable to trying to make the best creative use of information already obtained.

The idea of a festival of public relations – a week-long series of events in Leeds – was originated using this working-back technique. As Chair of the Chartered Institute of Public Relations (Yorkshire Group), I was pondering the problem of how we could reach practitioners who were 'outside the loop' (for unless you were a member you did not get to know about the Institute's activities). While sitting in a traffic jam in Leeds city centre musing on this question, I looked upon a giant 50-foot-long banner outside the Town Hall promoting a music festival in the city. 'What we could do with is a big banner like that about ourselves. What would we need to do to have a banner like that?' This was followed by further incremental thoughts, leading to the idea of a series of events that together could constitute a festival and would then justify the use of a giant banner. From this emerged a very successful promotion – and a very large banner proclaiming the work of the Institute.

State the problem in reverse

A variation on coming up with the Extreme Option is to state the problem in reverse, by changing a positive statement into a negative one. For example, if you are dealing with customer service as an issue, you could look at how you might make customer service *bad*. This flip-flopping of your perspective is a useful technique if you have difficulty in starting to think up new ideas, and it should

help to get you to develop further incremental ideas. It automatically gets you to suspend judgement and look at new combinations of ideas.

Create an imaginary person

In public relations work, we are often faced with situations where we are called upon to make a value judgement – of how a target audience may perceive an item, or how we should respond. This can be a difficult one to address, particularly in a crisis.

One trick is to create an imaginary person, possibly based on someone in real life, and you ask 'What would they think about this?' This was a technique used by Sir Bernard Ingham while he was Margaret Thatcher's press spokesman. Whenever he had to face what he regarded as esoteric questions from lobby journalists, he used to say: 'I have to tell you that is not the first topic of conversation in the "Two Ferrets" at Hebden Bridge.' It tended to shut them up and make the more sensitive feel precious. The 'Two Ferrets' is, of course, entirely a figment of the imagination, but that has not stopped tourists looking for it in Hebden Bridge. George Bernard Shaw also used this technique: he created an imaginary woman to whom he was writing as a means of overcoming writer's block. (He entitled one of his books *The Intelligent Woman's Guide to Socialism and Capitalism* in tribute to this imaginary reader.)

This technique is a vital creative tool in crises. For example, in 1996 I was called in at very short notice by Calderdale District Council to advise how it should handle a press conference to deal with its response to a Government Education Inspectorate report on the Ridings School in Halifax, which appeared to be damning. Complaints had been made about the behaviour of the pupils and that the school was out of control. The crisis had featured in a BBC *Panorama* programme and the media were describing the Ridings as 'the school from Hell'.

The Conservative Education Secretary of the time, Gillian Shephard, was calling a press conference in London that morning to give her view of the report and was certain to use the opportunity to criticize the Labour-run council in Calderdale. The members and officers felt under intense pressure, and advice was needed on a suitable statement to provide their response to this situation. Throughout this crisis I created in my mind a notional target of whom we should be tailoring our message for, focusing

my thoughts on parents of pupils at the school who wanted a normal and decent education for their children. There was a very vivid picture in my head of what parents would want to hear, what should be said to them, and what they would like to see done.

I thought the parents would welcome a team of experts closely scrutinizing their school. So the council was advised to welcome the Inspectorate's findings. I also reckoned the parents would not want to see squabbling and in-fighting, with what they would perceive as bureaucrats trying to hide or shift responsibility. The council was urged to accept its share of the blame for the situation – the tactic was to bottom-out the crisis, to try and get everything out of the way as soon as possible in order to avoid the affair dragging on. My notional target audience did not want just words or platitudes but to see something done. I devised what was labelled a '10-point Action Plan', which packaged together a number of activities that the council was planning to undertake and some further points that we felt necessary. When I was outlining my recommendations, someone replied: 'But we don't have a 10-point Action Plan.' 'Well, you have now', I said.

Snakes and ladders

Here is a good technique that helps use of the incremental nature of creativity to quickly establish an overview of a situation, identifying strengths and weaknesses, and to establish tactics to improve the positives and reduce the negatives.

Draw a grid on a sheet of paper to represent the squares of a snakes and ladders board. Imagine the objective of the task is at the top left-hand corner on the winning square. You are at the start, at the bottom right-hand corner. Draw in five short ladders and five long snakes. The snakes and ladder board should be drawn in seconds. The objective can be anything from: 'How can I improve the relationship between myself and the client or company senior management?' to profound questions such as: 'What shall I do with the rest of my life?'

Ask yourself the question: 'What five things would help me get closer to achieving my objective?' Now label each of your ladders with one of these five positive points. Next ask yourself: 'What five things are holding me back or are likely to get in the way of my achieving my objective?' This time label each of your five snakes with one of these five negatives. Now for each of the ladders say to yourself: 'What could I do to make this ladder longer and help me

get nearer my objective?' followed by: 'What could I do to make the snakes smaller so as to limit their ability to stop me reaching my goal?'

This is an excellent way of getting a handle on everything you need to consider. It also facilitates incremental thought as you come up with ideas to extend or minimize the particular issues. This technique also helps examine the detail of a situation and can be completed within a few minutes. An example is given in Figure 5.2.

Figure 5.2 *Use of the 'snakes and ladders' technique for a new product launch*

Forced combinations

The Matrix Technique can help practitioners generate 36 ideas in 36 seconds. By creating a matrix with six different variables down each side, you have 36 permutations. This is a particularly useful technique where there are known elements. Typical applica-

tions for practitioners include publicity press photocalls and the generation of ideas for names, such as for buildings or products.

A creative matrix for a photocall (shown in Table 5.1) could include on one side the often used ceremonies of a tape cutting, a tree planting (or sod turning), the unveiling of a plaque, a gift presentation, a handshake (or toast, or document signing), and the use of a prop (or other signage) involving the organization's products. On the other side of the matrix, six commonly used types of people taking part in these events could be listed – for example, the local mayor, a sports celebrity, the managing director, the oldest employee, a child, or a showbiz celebrity. Obviously, you can add extra names or activities or be more specific in your own matrix.

Table 5.1 *A matrix for a photocall*

	Tape cutting	Tree planting	Plaque unveiling	Gift presentation	Handshake	Prop
Mayor	Mayor cutting tape	Mayor planting tree	Mayor unveiling plaque	Mayor receiving gift	Mayor shaking hands	Mayor with prop
Sporting celebrity	Sports star cutting tape	Sports star planting tree	Sports star unveiling plaque	Sports star receiving gift	Sports star shaking hands	Sports star with prop
Managing Director	MD cutting tape	MD planting tree	MD unveiling plaque	MD receiving gift	MD shaking hands	MD with prop
Oldest employee	Oldest employee cutting tape	Oldest employee planting tree	Oldest employee unveiling plaque	Oldest employee receiving gift	Oldest employee shaking hands	Oldest employee with prop
Child	Child cutting tape	Child planting tree	Child unveiling plaque	Child receiving gift	Child shaking hands	Child with prop
Showbiz celebrity	Showbiz star cutting tape	Showbiz star planting tree	Showbiz star unveiling plaque	Showbiz star receiving gift	Showbiz star shaking hands	Showbiz star with prop

By using this matrix, 36 different combinations are instantly available for use.

This method can be used just as easily for coming up with ideas

for the name of a new object, such as a building. In the example in Table 5.2, we are using the name of a fictitious company – Overton Engineering of Wakefield, Yorkshire, started by a Mr George Harvey. Down the side are a number of themes that could be used to generate ideas for the first name and across the top are commonly used descriptions to accompany it.

Table 5.2 *A matrix for naming a building*

	Building	Tower	Plaza	House	Mansion	Lodge
Name of company	Overton Building	Overton Tower	Overton Plaza	Overton House	Overton Mansion	Overton Lodge
Location	Wakefield Building	Wakefield Tower	Wakefield Plaza	Wakefield House	Wakefield Mansion	Wakefield Lodge
Founder	Harvey Building	Harvey Tower	Harvey Plaza	Harvey House	Harvey Mansion	Harvey Lodge
Product themes	Engineering Building	Engineering Tower	Engineering Plaza	Engineering House	Engineering Mansion	Engineering Lodge
Aspiration themes	Cutting Edge Building	Cutting Edge Tower	Cutting Edge Plaza	Cutting Edge House	Cutting Edge Mansion	Cutting Edge Lodge
Enterprise themes	Precision Building	Precision Tower	Precision Plaza	Precision House	Precision Mansion	Precision Lodge

If you were to add another dimension with a further six elements, it would be possible to generate some 216 ideas by cross-referencing the different dimensions. And the idea can be taken even further by listing the different attributes in columns rather than in a matrix, as shown in Table 5.3.

Through the combination of different elements across each of the columns, a host of new opportunities may emerge. In the shaded examples of Table 5.3, the idea of the Managing Director planting a tree on top of the building to highlight the message of being a landmark for the company is produced. (There is no guarantee that every idea produced by this method will have merit!)

This technique is not suitable where there is only one solution and where time could best be served focusing on the particular issue. Nonetheless, it can be very useful, particularly for photocalls, for generating in a very short space of time a large number of

Table 5.3 *Listing of attributes*

Ceremonies	Celebrities	Location	Message
Tape cutting	Mayor	Front of building	New era for company
Tree planting	Sports celebrity	Top of building	No change for company
Plaque unveiling	Managing Director	In foyer	Landmark for company
Gift	Oldest employee	Unusual part of building	Celebration of success
Handshake	Child	In front of city landmark	Commitment to customers, etc
Prop	Showbiz celebrity	In front of company sign	New products

different permutations and for creating new relationships of different elements to explore and consider.

Random-word technique

When they first encounter it, most creativity course delegates are very sceptical of the random-word technique. However, such scepticism is very quickly dispelled.

The technique essentially consists of choosing a word at random. Looking through a newspaper is the best way of selecting a word. Choose a page number at random, then move your hand blindly around the page until you are instructed (or choose) to stop. The word or image at your fingertip is the chosen one. If your finger stops on a photograph, you simply use the specific item your finger is resting on – if, for example, it is a picture of a person and your finger has stopped on their shoulder, you should use the word 'shoulder'.

It is a good technique to use either by yourself or in small groups. Once, we used this technique to help a course delegate who had to come up with ideas for a forthcoming medical

conference on heart disease. The course was held during the height of the Balkan crisis in 1999 and the word chosen at random by one group was 'Serbia'. Initially perplexed, the group quickly come up with connecting ideas, such as 'Strategic strike on heart disease', 'War on heart disease', etc. Another group had the word 'house'. They came up with themes such as 'Heart disease in the home', 'Does the way we live lead to heart disease?', etc.

Very quickly – in the space of a few minutes – this technique will generate a range of new connections leading to either specific ideas or suggestions that may offer further scope for incremental development, and even new paradigms. The technique also has the advantage that, by producing a range of different creative themes and routes to explore, it avoids the tendency of people to close their Green Light thinking prematurely, come up with just one idea or theme and not explore other options.

The singer David Bowie also uses a similar technique in his songwriting in which he cuts different words from newspaper headlines and then matches them randomly to see what new ideas emerge.

A similar technique is to select an image at random. For example, you might be faced with the problem of coming up with new ideas about pensions and the random object chosen is, for example, a circle. You then start to think about connections and relationships between pensions and a circle to gain new insights.

The checklist (SCAMPER) technique

One of the pioneers of creative thinking, Alex Osborn, puts forward a checklist technique using a series of change words to compare with the situation at hand. A preferable version of this (because of its memorable acronym) is SCAMPER, devised by Michael Michalko, which stands for:

Substitute
Combine
Adapt
Modify (make bigger/smaller)
Put to other uses
Eliminate
Reverse

One of the change words is placed against the situation and the individual then thinks through the consequences for the task at hand.

A delegate on one of our creativity training courses, for example, used this technique to come up with a new way of demonstrating the potential of a new computer system about to be launched by his consultancy. By matching his task alongside the word 'Modify' he came up with the idea of using computer-enhanced photography to make the product one hundred times bigger, so as to create a very distinctive photograph.

An example of the value of making something smaller was the substantial national press coverage obtained when a new pub opened in Wakefield, Yorkshire. Nothing unusual in that except, against a trend for longer and later drinking hours, the landlord of 'Harry's Bar' sought a licence to close at 10 pm in order to create a special atmosphere in the pub.

From experience, creativity course delegates using the SCAMPER technique initially do not tend to feel comfortable using it. It is recommended that you practise and feel happy using the random-word techniques before harnessing a checklist method like SCAMPER.

The focusing method

In contrast with the Creative Range technique, the focusing method tries to get to the very heart of an issue by posing the question: 'What is the one key element within the situation we are working with?' The great advertising guru David Ogilvy describes the task thus in his book *Advertising* (Ogilvy, 1987): 'There is inherent drama in every product. Our number one job is to dig for it and capitalize upon it.' Or, as one elderly adman told me: 'You sell the sizzle not the steak.'

Attribute Listing or DNA Listing

A great technique for ensuring that all possible aspects of a problem are examined is Attribute Listing or DNA Listing. This helps to break down the problem into smaller and smaller bits and see what you then discover.

For example, if you were looking at the task of how to improve a firm's annual report, you could draw up a grid similar to the one in Table 5.4 in order to come up with ideas for producing a new

Table 5.4 *Example of Attribute Listing for a firm's annual report*

Components	Existing attributes	Potential ideas
Medium	Print	Internet, audio, video, etc
Print quality	Full colour throughout	Printing in black and white, company colours, etc
Images	Photographs	Line drawings, computer-generated imagery, etc
Photographs' subject matter	Board members, site locations	Products in use, customers, etc
Financial information	Stock Exchange minimum information	Breakdown of costs of key products, etc
Binding	Stapled, stitched	Bound with ribbons, metal bolts in hole-punched pages, etc

version. The publication has a number of components – the medium it uses, the quality of the printed material, various visual elements, its contents, and so on. Each component is identified and its existing attribute noted. Green Light thinking is then used to look at any potential new ideas for each specific attribute.

Attribute Listing is a useful technique for improvements in quality for complicated products, procedures or services. For public relations practitioners, it can allow a focus on one specific part, product, or process and also generate a wide range of ideas on details that could otherwise easily be overlooked.

Paradigm busting

A paradigm can be defined as providing a framework for the way we may view a situation. In facing the task of generating new

insights and new ideas, we may be faced with the need for help to get us out of the paradigm that is framing how we perceive a situation. There are a number of techniques to help what can be called 'paradigm busting'.

Although we use many methods of communication in our everyday life, when people face problem-solving situations they often narrow their perspective and fall into the trap of relying too heavily on one approach. How often do we kick ourselves when, looking back to a past problem, we say: 'If only I had approached it this way.' We can see we may have been too bound by certain assumptions in our analysis.

One way of approaching a problem with the paradigm-busting technique is to use different types of communication:

- *Visually*: we can use images, pictures, diagrams, drawings, illustrations, sketches, blueprints, or two- or three-dimensional representations, to represent the task at hand. (See also later references to mind mapping.)
- *Verbally*: words, text, sounds, and verbal alliterations can describe the problem. (The phrase used by the UK's Prime Minister, Tony Blair, in 1997, 'Tough on crime, tough on the causes of crime', could well have been created in this way.)
- *Numerically*: by using numbers and mathematics to explain the problem. (You may not know how to explain Einstein's theory of general relativity, but you may instantly recall his formula of $e = mc^2$.)
- *Sequentially*: while trying to find patterns in the information we are handling, new insights can be created. (Using this method I have on several occasions come up with ideas for presenting statistics to use in support of a client's case in a press release.)
- *Conceptually*: using symbols, theories, metaphors or analogies to generate new perspectives. (The best speech-writers know the power of metaphor in delivering a message, but this is not used enough in the writing of press releases.)
- *Emotionally*: through harnessing sentiments, feelings, passions or opinions, which can be effective in addressing situations. (In crisis PR, the most common mistake that practitioners make is to look at the facts rather than at the emotions. As a result, they often fail to manage all the dimensions of the problem).

Using a metaphor

People can be persuaded to look at something very familiar in a new way by the metaphor technique. For example, when we conduct 'awayday' sessions with clients, we play what we call 'The Restaurant Game'. The question posed is: 'If your company was a restaurant, what would it be like?' We then invite the client team to look at every aspect of its operation as if it was a restaurant. Is the service good? What sort of food is on offer – is it fast food or *haute cuisine*? What is the menu like – varied or standard? Are the staff attentive and friendly? The comparison is extended to cover every aspect of going to a restaurant.

It is possible to use other objects as a metaphor, such as 'If your company was a car, what would it be like?' The restaurant metaphor has nevertheless proved the most effective as every aspect of product, service, price, location and promotion is recognized and experienced by individual consumers.

The benefits of this technique are that it helps people gain an overview of their problem, enabling them to see the wood for the trees, while also helping to identify specific aspects of their company that need improving. By using a metaphor, the participants distance themselves from any internal politics and assumptions, and this helps them to suspend judgement and look at the detail of their situation.

PROVIDING A STRUCTURE TO INFORMATION GATHERING, IDEA CREATION AND THE EVALUATION OF IDEAS

Using six hats

Edward de Bono is perhaps the best-known writer on creativity and has developed techniques such as his 'Six Hats' method. This breaks down the thought process into structured stages, notably information gathering, idea generation, and critical evaluation.

Each stage is marked by a different coloured 'Hat'. This designates, in a very disciplined way, how the creative thoughts of an individual or group are focused on specific functions:

1. *The White Hat stage*, at the outset, focuses on information needs.

There is a strict rule of not disputing any contrary details; they are merely placed alongside each other.

2. *The Red Hat stage* represents fire and warmth and feelings. The idea is to think of any emotions, intuitions and hunches about the task and express them as they are.

3. *The Black Hat* is the stage for caution, risk assessment and criticism, where the emphasis is on what can go wrong.

4. *The Yellow Hat stage,* in contrast to the earlier stages, is characterized by a logical, positive look at the task and looking in parallel for benefits and values.

5. *The Green Hat* is where judgement is suspended and the creative effort is focused on the search for alternatives and new ideas, where attention is concerned with any possibility.

6. *The Blue Hat* is the 'blue sky' stage, which aims to establish an overview and seeks to orchestrate the thinking process.

The benefits of this approach are manifold. The main advantage is that it sets a discipline, particularly for group meetings, of taking one stage of the creative process at a time. Normally, we try to do everything at once, but the Six Hats approach allows us to focus on one thing at a time. Also, by establishing a discipline it does shorten meetings. IBM, it is claimed, found it reduced meeting times by 75 per cent.

On an individual level, the opportunity to switch thinking habits encourages flexibility. From experience, when you involve management teams in creative brainstorming sessions, the normally dour company accountants, the habitual Black Hat thinkers, tend to surprise their colleagues by abandoning negative thinking.

Organizing you thoughts and new creative ideas

Mind mapping, devised by Tony Buzan, is another much-publicized method of using the way you present information to provide a structure to thinking. It also encourages incremental thought.

Read any of Tony Buzan's books on the subject; all are interesting and good fun. Here is a brief step-by-step guide to your own mind-map making, and a mind map of making mind maps is shown in Figure 5.3. There are five basic steps to the process:

1. Start with a drawing to act as a central image. Make your map as beautiful as possible and ideally use at least three colours. This helps you generate a sense of pride in the task and brings a sense of commitment, in contrast with the feelings generated from a scruffy composition of jottings.

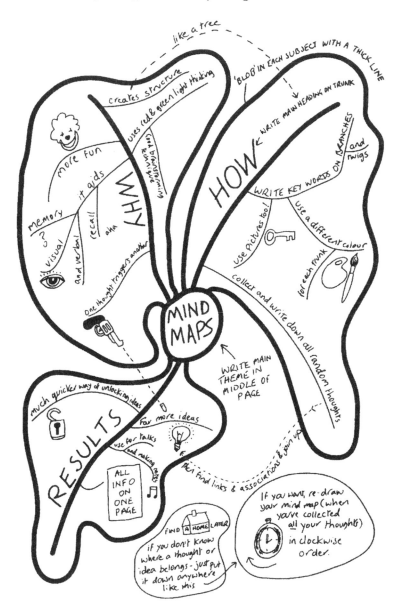

Figure 5.3 *A mind map on how to do mind maps*

2. From the central image, order your thoughts so that they radiate out with lines in the sequence of their importance. Any key words should be emphasized by printing them in capital letters on these lines. Remember to use only one word per line and to keep the letters upright. Use your favourite colours to emphasize different key words.
3. Highlight the importance of the different thoughts by varying the thickness of lines, and use spacing.
4. Show further connections between your thoughts by connecting lines to each other, linking and associating ideas with loops, curves and arrows. You can also use symbols, such as happy or sad faces, to illustrate any positive or negative points.
5. Help your memory by using graphic elements or words relating to the senses wherever possible.

This technique is particularly helpful when dealing with complex situations where there is a need to set priorities. The strong use of visuality is also effective in making the issues and ideas memorable for easier recall.

Idea and Problem Bank

When looking at the Illumination stage of the creative process, we saw how people fail to record all the ideas that come to mind. You should write down or record as many Illumination thoughts as possible. But it is not always possible to make immediate use of these ideas and sometimes you will want help from others.

One solution is to create your own Idea and Problem Bank. This is a place where you can submit problems to be solved by others. Problems can be deposited in the bank and withdrawn by other people, to be returned with possible solutions. For example, public relations consultancy Communique uses its internal e-mail system to circulate ideas and problems.

TECHNIQUES FOR ENCOURAGING A CREATIVE STATE OF MIND

Here are a number of techniques that you can use to encourage your mind to be creative.

The Disney strategy

A technique inspired by Walt Disney uses a set of distinct stages to encourage creativity and certain states of mind for each stage of the creative process.

First, there is a 'Dreamer' stage. Here you visualize a place in front of you to step into. You literally become a dreamer and are completely free to brainstorm – to create without any restraints. While you are here, think back to a time when you generated some creative choices. Step into the spot and relive the experience as fully and immediately as you can. By doing this you associate, or anchor, the dreamer, the creative part of your mind, to that spot. Step out when finished.

This is followed by a 'Realist' stage, in which you choose a different place to become a 'realist'. You need to sift the dreams, organize them and act upon them.

You need to know how dreams are translated into the real world. Think of a time when you thought realistically and constructively about an idea and devised an effective action plan. Step inside this spot and relive that experience. Anchor the realist part of you to that spot and, when satisfied, step out.

Lastly, the 'Critic' stage is where you select a place to be a critic or to evaluate. Think of a time when you were able to criticize a plan in a constructive way. Again, step out.

Now you have created three places, or states of mind, as 'anchors' for a particular thought process and you can visit and revisit all three places at any time. With its use of anchor points, this technique is helpful in creating a suitable state of mind for generating ideas. (See Chapter 13.)

Stand up, Incubation Rest, low-cortical-awareness break

After 40 minutes or so in a meeting, simply get everyone to stand up and, as Jane Austen would say, 'do a turn around the room'. Attempt anything different, even just looking out of the window. (One company encourages its staff to play with Lego building blocks.) If you are in a meeting, swap places. This will not only give you the chance to freshen up but will also help you look at a situation literally from a new perspective.

Some great writers testify to the merits of giving yourself a break and a change of activity, from going out for a walk, or relaxing in a bath, to taking exercise. This gives them what we have called an

Incubation Rest, or a low-cortical-awareness break, during which further Illuminations are likely to emerge.

Affirmations

Affirmations provide a useful method of 'programming' your mind to act in a particular way. These work by creating a positive statement about yourself and then repeating it regularly. You can have your specific affirmations produced on cards and even as reminders on your computer.

Affirmations can work for individuals and for groups. Typical affirmations for an individual are as follows:

- I am a successful public relations practitioner.
- I am willing to use my creative talents.
- I have a constant flow of new and interesting ideas.
- I treat each new problem that I encounter as a new door to be opened, and an opportunity to be creative.
- Through the use of a few simple tools, my creativity will flourish.

Before you think of this technique as too far-fetched, with an image of group hugs and mantra chants, consider the effective leaders and managers that you have known. They have very likely succeeded by getting their teams to share a common vision and belief, although actually proclaiming their affirmations in a subtle or non-overt manner.

Alcohol and drugs

Are alcohol or drugs useful as stimulants to creativity? Stories of people appearing to come up with a great idea after a few drinks are commonplace. Yet, if you look at the elements of these situations, the drinks and drugs are conducive to creativity only in that judgement is being suspended, sometimes coupled with the benefits of social situations where you are more likely to be relaxed and free of immediate work pressures. These ingredients are better described as influential factors rather than the effects of the substances. (Besides, there is the catch-22 of not being able to remember any good ideas when you are drunk, until you get drunk again!)

The great surrealist artist André Breton derided the potential benefits of drugs to inspire his art when he declared: 'Surrealism is

the intoxication.' Likewise, when you are in full flow, freely coming up with ideas is the best fix for any creative public relations practitioner.

 Try as many of the techniques described in this chapter as you can in order to generate ideas on future assignments. You will soon find the ones that work best for you, or are more suitable for particular tasks.

You may know of, or come across, other techniques for generating ideas. Examine how they achieve any of the following. Do they:

1. *suspend judgement or perspectives;*
2. *stimulate a quantity of ideas;*
3. *focus on the detail of a situation or problem;*
4. *generate combinations of different elements;*
5. *give a structure or discipline to your information gathering, idea creation, and evaluation of a situation;*
6. *encourage a creative state of mind;*
7. *enable the individual to detach from any anxieties involved in being creative about the task being faced;*
8. *create time to be creative?*

SUMMARY

1. Although many experienced practitioners may appear to be intuitively creative, their creative ideas are the product of their using a technique, albeit subconsciously.
2. Failing to separate the use of Green Light and Red Light thinking can lead to Brown Light thinking (where the resulting ideas are of poor quality, of limited originality, or where valuable time and other resources are used inefficiently).
3. Any techniques for generating ideas will achieve one, or more, of eight key tasks.
4. Never having enough time to be creative is not a valid excuse.

KEY WORDS FOR YOUR CREATIVITY VOCABULARY

- Anchoring.
- Attribute.
- Extreme option.
- Low cortical awareness.
- Mind map.
- Safe bet.

6

Green Light thinking: brainstorming

> We tried brainstorming once, but nothing came from it. All we got was a lot of far-out ideas.
>
> *A not uncommon response to a suggestion for a brainstorming session*

Mention the subject of creativity or the task of coming up with ideas, and one word usually comes to mind: brainstorming. 'Let's brainstorm this one' is usually the cue within public relations departments and consultancies trying to come up with new ideas and insights. This chapter puts brainstorming into the context of Green Light thinking techniques and shows how public relations practitioners can use brainstorming effectively.

The word 'brainstorming' is often used as an umbrella term to describe the process of being creative. In the context of this book, the word is solely concerned with describing a formal group technique to generate new ideas.

There is an urban myth circulating that the word 'brainstorming' is not politically correct and you should not use it as it offends people with epilepsy or mental illness. Other words that could be used instead include 'thought showering'. This is

absolute nonsense. Each year I conduct a survey with leading campaign and charity groups connected with either epilepsy or mental health. None have policies against the use of the word 'brainstorming'. If you come across anyone raising an objection to using the word 'brainstorm' or circulating the myth in any way, please put them straight.

GENERAL PRINCIPLES

Brainstorming is perhaps the most well-known creativity technique. It was pioneered by Alex Osborn in the 1950s, in his seminal book *Applied Imagination* (Osborn, 1953). The dictionary defines brainstorming as: 'practising a conference technique by which a group attempts to find a solution for a specific problem by amassing all the ideas spontaneously contributed by its members'. Osborn argued that it is possible deliberately to increase the production of good ideas by following two principles, namely the deferment of judgement and a quantity of ideas breeding quality.

The rules of brainstorming, as defined by Osborn, are as follows:

- Brainstormers are placed in an informal setting.
- Brainstormers are encouraged to run wild intellectually.
- No one should criticize anyone else's idea.
- The more unusual or crazy the idea the better.
- The more suggestions the better.
- Ideas can be combined and recombined.
- All brainstormers' views are sought.
- All brainstormers are of equal status.

Osborn argues that the optimum number for a brainstorming group is 12. An ideal panel should consist of a leader, an associate leader, about 5 regular (or core) members, and about 5 guests. Overall, an odd number in the group may be useful so as to provide scope for a clear majority in any subsequent discussion. The core members should act as pace-setters for the session. A regular change in the membership of the group is also thought useful, because the same group left together over a long period of time tends to develop a rigid pattern of thinking, with the danger that one member can anticipate the reactions of another.

Since Osborn first posulated his ideas for brainstorming, it has become the most common technique in creativity in the marketing services industry. However, it is not just a technique for groups; it is possible to apply the principles of brainstorming working by yourself. In any case, Osborn's recommended number of 12 participants is difficult to recreate in most UK in-house departments or consultancies.

The advantages of Osborn's style of brainstorming are thus:

- Time and effort arises from several people and therefore there is access to more information and skill.
- More ideas and more varied ideas are likely to be generated.
- Errors are more likely to be detected as more than one person is involved.
- By involving individual team members, brainstorming increases their commitment to any subsequent decisions.
- Brainstorming avoids the 'tepid water syndrome' (or what we have earlier called 'Brown Light thinking').

In connection with this last point, if you were to get hot and cold water out of a tap at the same time then you would end up with tepid water, and people likewise make the mistake of mixing up generating ideas with their evaluation. The two tasks should be quite distinct, and initially focusing solely on *generating* ideas advances the efforts to find a creative solution.

Brainstorming does, however, have disadvantages. Successful brainstorming is dependent upon having someone involved who 'owns' the problem, is accountable for it, wants to solve it, and has the power to do something about it. Brainstorming can also be a self-indulgent waste of time if the session tackles the wrong kind of problem or is unstructured. This latter is a point echoed by Graham Lancaster of Biss Lancaster when he said, when interviewed: 'Free-ranging creative brainstorming sessions tend, on the whole, to be a bad idea. People are always poorly briefed, and just throw around sparky ideas to show off – whether on strategy or not.' Brainstorming is not good in crisis situations where rapid decisions and clear leadership are needed. Nor is it good for clearly structured situations where there is a straightforward solution. Brainstorming works best on specific and limited – but open-ended – problems.

In any group there is a tendency for some members to be 'wall-

flowers' and hardly make any contribution, while a number of 'talkers' will emerge who take up a majority of the time with their ideas and views. A tip to tackle this problem is to include a 'pass' technique where each participant has to take part in a round-robin. If they cannot think of anything they say 'pass'.

The effects of status and power come into play where there are individuals of different rank within the organization who are present in the brainstorming session. Inevitably, pressures to conform, deference and organizational politics can then influence the extent to which people take part. Despite the ground rules of 'running wild intellectually', what may be seen as outrageous ideas could be derided and mocked, either verbally or – just as significantly – non-verbally.

People tend to judge ideas too soon, starting to evaluate suggestions during the brainstorming rather than using the session solely *to generate* new ideas. A key skill in brainstorming is to avoid reaching a premature evaluation or a conclusion too soon; once a conclusion is reached people begin to argue the case rather than looking for new insights. Avoid Red Light thinking in brainstorming. We can all recall occasions when one person puts an idea forward that then gets ridiculed, or where someone immediately goes into Red Light thinking mode and starts analysing the practical problems that they perceive as being connected to the idea.

For a brainstorming session to be successful, it is imperative that a process is established at the outset containing a definition of the task to be addressed, criteria for evaluating any ideas generated and resources and a timescale for putting these ideas and insights into action.

Brainstorming is not an end in itself. The technique throws up ideas. It doesn't offer a systematic problem-solving sequence to creating solutions. Most sessions do not establish a clear-cut system for subsequently evaluating ideas. As a result, people complain about the 'waste of time', with nothing to show for their labours, apparently having expected the brainstorming session to come up with answers there and then, rather than to generate new insights for *later* evaluation.

Research shows that group brainstorming is not as effective as individuals working by themselves; if individuals are left to come up with ideas, they are more likely to emerge with a greater number of higher-quality ideas. Think about how many times you have read a poem written by a committee. Green Light thinking

techniques (described in Chapter 5) are used by individuals or small groups of people, and are generally better than brainstorming techniques at generating new ideas. However, brainstorming has considerable value outside the arena of creativity through:

- enabling someone to overcome any personal anxieties about being creative by providing a means to involve other people, who can share the problem;
- team-building and staff development, because it provides the opportunity for members of a public relations team and different grades of staff to work together;
- acceptance of an idea by participation;
- formally putting creativity on other people's timetables: if a group of people is 'ordinarily' asked to come up with ideas, only one or two tend to make a serious contribution; the others either never get around to it or only put in a half-hearted effort;
- putting creativity on the medium-term agenda. Creativity is one of those issues that does not get on the phone and say: 'You're not being creative and have not scheduled sufficient time to be creative; nor have you carried out a creative review over the last six months.' As a formal technique, brainstorming helps register the need for more creativity sessions. 'When was the last time we had a brainstorm on this one?' is a call from the conscience that, sadly, can sometimes come too late.

A NEW WAY AHEAD: STRUCTURED BRAINSTORMING

In response to the working needs of public relations practitioners, I have developed 'Structured Brainstorming'. This technique demonstrates an understanding of the nature of creativity. It recognizes that creativity works incrementally, and harnesses both Green Light and Red Light thinking. It uses the creative process effectively and separates individual from group brainstorming (where solitary thinking is best for having ideas, and group thinking is best for building on these ideas).

Structured Brainstorming consists of nine steps, as set out in Figure 6.1 and described in more detail starting below.

Step 1

A senior manager

Step 2

Criteria are established

Step 3

An initial plan is devised

Steps 4 and 5

Green Light thinking –
brainstorming session

Brainstorm includes
a Scribe ...

... and a Cheerleader

Step 6

A day later collect
any further ideas

Step 7

Red Light thinking –
evaluating and judging ideas

Steps 8 and 9

Establish the plan and
gain acceptance

Figure 6.1 *A guide to Structured Brainstorming*

Step 1: A senior manager analyses the brief

Any creative element must be – and can only be – effective in a framework of defined objectives. Only by setting goals and providing a structure within which communication can take place

can you identify where added value from the creative process is needed. A framework also provides a measure to gauge the value – and, indeed, the commercial worth – of any subsequent creativity.

A senior member of staff analyses the brief and may also use Green Light thinking to focus on the information stage of the creative process: What sources of information are available? Are there any unusual places to look for potential sources of ideas? The senior member then works through the structured elements of a typical public relations programme:

- *Situation*: the task is described and put into context. The key outcome is stated as clearly as possible.
- *Problems*: what problems are raised by the brief that need solving? Use Green Light thinking to identify any further issues or problems to be solved, or look at making the problem more specific.
- *Objectives*: what you want to achieve. Again, use Green Light thinking to identify any new issues, adding further objectives as necessary.
- *Audiences*: the different groups you need to reach. You can be creative either by extending the number of target groups, or by being more specific and targeted.
- *Messages*: what you need to say. Look not just at the obvious statements in the brief, but examine how you can come up with new themes, messages and points of view.
- *Channels*: the different communication routes to your audiences.
- *Opportunities*: specific events or topical issues that could be used to advantage (and Chapter 13 describes 'surfing', namely adding value by linking with a topical event or issue). Here is a checklist that can be used to judge your activity against potential opportunities that may lend themselves to surfing. The checklist should also help you identify opportunities for linking, and for providing new creative ideas and added value:
 - seasonality – winter/spring/summer/autumn;
 - events – theme weeks/days, sport (forthcoming tournaments, or sports people in the news), politics (issues of current concern), exhibitions (forthcoming shows, trade events) or commemorative anniversaries;
 - topicality – films, television, arts or fashion;
 - VIPs – visits, endorsements or links with an organization;
 - the local area – cultural strengths/weaknesses.

- *Threats*: what could emerge to undermine your efforts, such as competitive activity, environmental developments, and also the consequences of inactivity – for instance, what would happen if you did not run your campaign?
- *Resources*: don't just assume your resources are confined to the budget allowed for in the brief, because creative thought can generate added funds, resources or assistance. Is there any third party or generic trade activity that can be piggybacked on to, or any sponsorship to provide more income? (You can win major industry awards with campaigns for which there was no budget, and organize celebrity photocalls without paying a penny for the celebrity, through using creative thinking on the available resources.)
- *Programme*: distil all the ideas into a coherent campaign, with deadlines.
- *Evaluation*: think up benchmarks and measures, working creatively.
- *Illustration*: what ideas will help to sell the programme?

Step 2: Criteria are established

Use Red Light thinking to establish criteria for evaluating ideas. See Chapter 8 for an expansion of this theme.

Step 3: An initial plan is devised

An initial plan is drafted as a proposal for action. If you need more ideas, circulate the draft to colleagues before the brainstorming session. They should read the draft as soon as possible, so as to capitalize on their incubation of ideas.

Steps 4 and 5: Green Light thinking – brainstorming session

Only at this stage should a brainstorming session be prepared for. You need one or two flipcharts, a variety of coloured pens, and a set of red and green cards. Hold the session in a room that accommodates everyone in comfort, offers privacy, is free from distractions, and away from interruptions such as telephones (especially mobile phones).

Timing is important. First thing in the morning should be avoided, when people may have the day's other commitments on their minds, as should after lunch, when body clocks are at a low ebb.

Group rapport is a fundamental prerequisite of successful brainstorming. If there is sufficient time, get people into a relaxed state of mind. Hold a warm-up game to tackle a hypothetical situation. For example: 'If you're stuck on a desert island, what uses can you make of a belt?' Even well-established teams with strong rapport find this stimulating.

The brainstorming session should have a clear structure. Appoint people to take the role of Cheerleader and Scribe. Make the rules explicit.

Have a Cheerleader to encourage and exhort the group, and to stay alert to any 'wallflowers' in order to make sure they participate fully. The Cheerleader should check the body language and watch out for non-verbal communication, encouraging everyone to be open, relaxed and non-threatening.

The Cheerleader is there to encourage the team to build upon ideas, so holds the red and green cards, encouraging participants with a few totally outrageous ideas. This demonstrates how everyone should suspend judgement and show there is no bar to creative thought. Use Green Light thinking; suspend judgement or evaluation. The Cheerleader shows a red card to anyone who is using Red Light judgements or negative thinking. Seek as many ideas as possible. Aim for frequency and quantity, not quality.

The Scribe notes down all suggestions made.

The suggested structure provides for a series of two-minute sessions, each focused on one aspect of the elements in the draft public relations programme. Start with a problems session, move on to objectives, audiences and so on, finishing at the illustration stage. Everyone should try to build upon each other's ideas. Stop after two minutes. Give the Scribe an extra 30 seconds to catch up and note down all the ideas. The number of ideas is recorded and noted. Then you start the next section.

If there are enough people – say eight or more – split the group into two or more teams to capitalize on people's inherent competitive spirit. The teams should either be in adjoining rooms or in different corners of the same room, so that they can work independently of each other. Compare team scores before the next session

starts. (For those who believe that people cannot get competitive in these situations, I have even seen teams whisper their ideas to their Scribe to lull the other team into a false sense of insecurity!)

At the outset, you should set a strict time limit and stick to it. The whole meeting can be completed in around 25 minutes. Do not spend much more time than this in any brainstorming session; it will be a waste of time, as people's brains get tired and distracted.

While people should be relaxed in brainstorming, they should not get too comfortable. You should make everyone stand up to do the brainstorm. This not only discourages people from sitting back and letting their minds wander off the subject, but also focuses them on the task in hand.

On our training courses, delegates have used the rhythm of their body to stimulate creative thoughts. One method, which can be called 'Doing the Bill', involves placing one foot in front of the other and gently rocking backwards and forward, seeking with every forward lean to come up with an idea. Alternatively, 'Doing the Fiona' consists of jumping up and down on the spot to generate new thoughts. This, however, is a bit wearing on the legs – and on the carpet.

Step 6: A day later collect any further ideas

Next day, the coordinator follows up with each participant and asks everyone to note down in no more than 30 seconds – in order not to take up too much time – any other ideas that have emerged since the structured brainstorm. This capitalizes on the incubation stage, because what invariably happens is that the brainstorming stimulates new thoughts and ideas after the session. Unless this follow-up is carried out, these extra ideas are lost.

Step 7: Red Light thinking – evaluating and judging ideas

Place the criteria (established in Step 2) alongside the ideas noted. Rather than subjectively evaluating individual ideas, the criteria help to introduce an objective appraisal. (See Chapter 8 on Red Light thinking.)

Step 8: Establish the plan

Now establish a programme using some of the ideas. You may even redefine the problem. Include deadlines and measures of success. Give a copy of the programme to everyone who took part in the original brainstorm, in order to provide feedback on their input.

Step 9: Gain acceptance

The illustration stage of the creative process is brought into play as it is vital to gain acceptance from those affected by the proposed solution.

Some alternative Structured Brainstorming ideas

Instead of using a Scribe, you can self-scribe by using self-adhesive notes. Either by yourself, or in groups of ideally no more than four people, you write one idea per note and place it on a flipchart sheet.

Self-scribing has a number of advantages. By writing down your ideas you may feel less inhibited. As you are using a non-verbal way of expressing ideas it also is a way of managing 'shouters' who would otherwise dominate the session. Posting the sticky notes on to a group sheet also provides an opportunity to look at other people's ideas and generate connections and further ideas from them.

One technique to use is a '60-second soapbox'. This consists of giving every participant a notional 60 seconds to write down ideas they already have. This has two advantages; firstly it is a very time-efficient means for capturing a body of ideas people already have. Secondly, it enables people to get their own pet ideas down, so they can then have a free mind, without any baggage of existing ideas, to generate new insights and permutations.

In practice this usually takes 2–4 minutes for each set question you are sparking ideas on. You should always continue until your energy or the group's energy is dissipated. When you are feeling mentally dried out, give yourself one last push. Experience has shown that you tend to get your best quality ideas when you think you have no more to give. You can also get a facilitator to give you false deadlines to stimulate the sense of no more to give. Do not

however waste time sitting around in frustrating sessions trying to force ideas out. Maintain a high energy level and move on to different techniques either to spark further ideas or consolidate the ideas you are generating.

You should then begin a 'chunking exercise' to group ideas which are either the same or have a similar theme or subject matter. Typically, a group may have generated between 30–40 ideas in the 60-second soapbox. Aim for a target of five chunks.

Once you have established your chunks give each of them a name. Aim to be as specific as possible in describing your chunk. You then need to build a question around the chunk name. In one example a group had created chunks around the following themes: 'Internal communications', 'Promotional ideas', 'Messages', 'External resources', and 'Leader's personality'.

Translating these into subsequent questions the group created the following: 'How can we improve internal communications?', 'What specific promotional techniques can we identify?', 'What specific messages do we need to create?', 'What external resources can we identify to help in our task?', 'What aspects of the leadership's personality can we use in this campaign?'

When you are Green Light thinking you are generating thoughts to create banks of ideas and questions.

An overview

It should be clear from the foregoing description of the nine steps to Structured Brainstorming that it offers the following to users:

- a system that is more time efficient, and pinpoints the creative needs of the situation;
- use of the incubation process, both before and after the group brainstorming sessions;
- benefits in team building, where staff development is encouraged through junior and senior members working together and where team competitiveness can be harnessed to generate ideas;
- a focus on problem solving, and procedures to help concentrate the minds of everyone taking part;
- encouragement to take part again, by offering involvement and feedback.

NOMINAL GROUP TECHNIQUE (NGT)

Another technique, for which I am indebted to the Chartered Institute of Public Relations Mind Link Group (which promotes a greater understanding of the use of psychology in public relations), is the Nominal Group Technique, commonly referred to as NGT. This has been developed by Delbecq, Van de Ven and Gustafson.

The name 'Nominal Group Technique' reflects the fact that individuals working as individuals are actually more effective than a group, and in using NGT they are in many ways a group in name only.

The six stages

The NGT consists of six distinct problem-solving stages, summarized in Table 6.1 and described in more detail thus:

- *Stage 1: Generate ideas.* This first stage involves the silent generation of ideas by individuals, who write them down.
- *Stage 2: Share ideas.* Individuals come together in the group to collect ideas on a round robin of one idea from each person, each round. A 'pass' technique can be used until all the ideas are submitted.
- *Stage 3: Clarify and develop the ideas.* All the ideas that have been collected are discussed in the group. Individuals explain their submitted ideas in turn, without interruption.
- *Stage 4: Select the best idea.* A preliminary secret vote takes place on the relative importance of ideas, using ranking, rating or voting systems.
- *Stage 5: Check the decisions.* Individuals now have the chance to argue again for their ideas if they have been discarded.
- *Stage 6: Confirm/modify the decisions.* A final secret vote is taken.

With NGT it is important to maintain discipline, and individuals must confine themselves to the requirements of the particular stage. For example, in Stage 2 ideas should be merely labelled and not described; the ideas can be described during Stage 3.

The majority of experiments have shown that when brainstorming groups are compared with individuals using brainstorming-type instructions, individuals rather than groups produce the

Table 6.1 *A stage-by-stage guide to the Nominal Group Technique*

Stage number	Stage description
Stage 1	Generate ideas
Stage 2	Share ideas
Stage 3	Clarify and develop the ideas
Stage 4	Select the best idea
Stage 5	Check the decision
Stage 6	Confirm/modify the decisions

more creative ideas. Techniques such as NGT use the independent work of individuals to generate ideas.

The ideas generated are pooled systematically and without losses. Using a round robin allows everyone to build on and 'spark off' the ideas of others, increasing group productivity. The co-ordination of individuals is improved, and participation is equalized. Having a well-defined set of rules means 'the amount you talk' and 'the amount you have to say' are much more closely related than in normal *ad hoc* brainstorming groups.

The stages of idea generation, of idea clarification and development, and of idea evaluation are separated. Thus the premature rejection of ideas – and thus the failure to consider them all – and the premature acceptance of ideas are prevented.

The decision-making procedure is clear. Depending on the nature of the problem, different procedures can be used as agreed and as appropriate. Built into all of them is the discipline of re-examining the decision taken. Any differences are identified by anomalies and 'splits' in the voting, and these differences must be discussed and resolved before any final decision can be taken.

By using NGT, pressures to conform are eliminated, or at least minimized, through the use of secret voting. This eliminates individual pressures for consistency (which hinders the ability to change your mind in the light of new information).

The person who takes the chair in the group meeting acts simply as a coordinator. The Chair's concern is with procedure, therefore minimizing conflicts of role.

The procedure can be used repeatedly, initially to identify and define the problem to be solved. It can then be used to schedule

potential solutions, and then to plan action and evaluation. The procedure can also be readily subdivided, with each stage forming a natural point at which to adjourn.

SUMMARY

1. Brainstorming is just one among many techniques for generating ideas. It is not suitable for all problem-solving tasks.
2. Individuals working alone are better at generating ideas. Brainstorming is a good group technique for building upon ideas.
3. Techniques described in Chapter 5, used either by individuals or small groups of people, are better at generating new ideas than brainstorming.
4. Brainstorming has value outside the arena of creativity: in team-building, staff development, and in gaining acceptance of ideas.
5. 'Structured Brainstorming' is a highly effective creative technique.
6. You can hold a meeting using NGT and no one outside the room will know.
7. If you are in a brainstorming session lasting more than 45 minutes, leave the room.

KEY WORDS FOR YOUR CREATIVITY VOCABULARY

- Brown Light thinking.
- Cheerleader.
- Premature evaluation.
- Rapport.
- Scribe.
- Structured brainstorming.
- Wallflower.

7

Creativity – the consultation tool

Don't ask what we can do for you, or what you can do for us; ask what can we do together

A consultation mantra

This is a story about one of the all-time greats of advertising, Rosser Reeves – the man who first came up with the concept of the unique selling proposition – USP.

During one warm New York spring he and a colleague decided to have lunch in Central Park. Finishing their sandwiches they strolled back to the office on Madison Avenue. On the sidewalk a beggar stood, holding a sign and a cup for donations. Everyone ignored him. His sign read: 'I am blind.'

Witnessing this scene Reeves said to his colleague: 'He's using the wrong message; I bet I can dramatically improve the response to him with just a few words.' The wager on, Rosser explained to the beggar that he was one of the United States' greatest copy-writers and he would like to help him. Perhaps feeling he had nothing to lose, the beggar agreed to let Rosser rewrite his sign.

Stepping well back, Rosser and his colleague observed this live

experiment in the effects of message and copy on response. Instantly, passers-by saw the new sign and then stopped, looked up at the sky around them and then got their wallet or purse out to make a donation.

What did Rosser write? (Think about it before reading on.)

Rosser used a tactic of establishing commonality with his audience. Taking his own feelings, enjoying the pleasures of a spring day, as a cue he wrote on the sign: 'It is springtime'.

The fundamental communications lesson is how you need to work back from the reality of where people are, rather than from your world view, your reality, to engage effectively. Presumably, passers-by could relate and empathize with the blind man's situation, in contrast to their earlier, distant response to his pleas.

Taking this principle further, if you start your communications from where people are and then involve and engage them in your plans you will dramatically improve the prospects for gaining acceptance and buying in to your goals.

Communications is not just about relaying information, it is a tool for creating change. If you can creatively identify different ways to engage, involve and create a dialogue with different stakeholders you can dramatically improve the effectiveness of your communications. By involving and engaging people in a process you can dramatically enhance their performance. The very act of involvement is crucial to gaining acceptance.

Consultation is a well-established tool formally used in central and local government planning processes. Yet it has far more potential for modern-day creative communicators to create impact and secure sustainable change.

Working in an era of increasing media fragmentation and speed of communications consultation can be described as a form of social networking – an offline activity.

Ultimately, at some point in most communications campaigns you have to meet people face to face. A creatively well-designed consultation activity can deliver a relevant opportunity to your target market and offer an optimum experience in their dialogue or relationship with you.

Consultation can be defined as an equation:

Consultation = get the right people + listen + demonstrate you have listened

Similarly, the benefits of consultation can be defined as:

Good consultation = insight + engagement + mutual respect

Creative public relations practitioners can use their flexible thinking tools to:

- identify different audiences to be consulted;
- engage hard-to-reach audiences;
- overcome initial objections;
- obtain political buy-in from key targets;
- express and make a statement about their own creativity through creative consultation;
- generate new ideas and alternative solutions from those being consulted;
- obtain valuable market intelligence and insight;
- create super-advocates for their cause.

IDENTIFY DIFFERENT AUDIENCES TO BE CONSULTED

The first task in undertaking a consultation exercise is to identify who will be impacted by a decision or campaign, and also who can influence how a communication will be received.

Creative thinking can help you look beyond the obvious groups to involve in your consultation. There can also be a tendency to oversimplify target groups, making assumptions to create broad-brush descriptions of target groups, which could actually mask different sub-groups, with a distinct view or response to your activity.

 What assumptions have you made about a target audience you were seeking to reach?

ENGAGE HARD-TO-REACH AUDIENCES

With a growing importance of putting people at the heart of health and social care, it is vital to involve citizens in planning the

services they want. Yet how do you effectively engage with people who are apparently not able to conduct 'meaningful' engagement?

Chris Dabbs is a futurologist with significant experience in engaging people in health and social care issues. He believes with creative thought and persistence even the most apparently vulnerable people can be reached. Working with people with dementia (a group of different brain disorders involving a loss of brain function that is usually progressive), he has sought their own voices.

The onus is on believing they have a voice, facilitating it, and then hearing it. As far as possible, one must enter and accept their world on their terms. Chris found that, as with all people, having repeated low expectations of people with dementia created disempowerment and 'learned helplessness'. He says:

> If you were sat in a chair day after day with little stimulation or communication about your skills and interests, you would steadily give up trying and become depressed. Dementia is only an impairment. Most people with it are disabled only by disempowering, insensitive attitudes and actions from others.

Chris found that the top priorities for people with dementia were issues around personal and social relationships, occupation and activities, and psychological and emotional health.

> People with dementia deserve the dignity and respect that everyone expects for themselves. They have at least as much to offer others as others might offer them. If they are allowed to contribute as partners, not only will services become more effective but their quality of life will improve.

The challenge is not how to 'manage' people with dementia, but to accept that we all have deficiencies, to challenge one's own anxieties and defences, and to really listen to what people are seeking to communicate.

OVERCOME INITIAL OBJECTIONS

In some instances a public relations campaign can start on the back foot, with a vested opposition raised about a plan before you may chance to formally begin your own communications plan.

Campaigns for supporting a planning application are often best served by making a few informal calls with key targets before embarking on any formal communications programme. I once visited a local group of the Institute of Advanced Motorists with a sponsorship proposal from a new motor dealer client. The degree of animosity that greeted me on arrival cannot be understated. It appeared the group had repeatedly received very rude treatment when they had previously approached the dealer for sponsorship requests.

I adopted a position of apologizing but then asking: 'What is it you would really like?' From this starting point it was possible to establish a dialogue and a positive relationship grew from the shakiest of starts.

OBTAIN POLITICAL BUY-IN FROM KEY TARGETS

One of the key benefits of brainstorming is its ability to obtain political buy-in from participants. By taking part in a brainstorm you are more likely to be bought-in to the subsequent outcomes. If you are faced with an individual or groups who constantly knock-back ideas engage them in the brainstorm. Being part of the process legitimizes the subsequent output of the brainstorm.

Have you been involved in a campaign where you failed to obtain the political buy-in of a key target?

EXPRESS AND MAKE A STATEMENT ABOUT YOUR OWN CREATIVITY

In some instances you need to demonstrate your own creativity by delivering your consultation in an original fashion.

Below is the format of an event devised for Theatre Royal and Opera House, Wakefield for a consultation exercise with key stakeholders on the draft strategic plan devised by the theatre Board. The format was designed to accommodate information giving and briefing but crucially coupled with activities to solicit views, ideas and responses.

Within the time available the focus of the consultation was centred on three key questions designed to identify the significance of the Theatre in the local community, comments on the draft

Time	Activity	By
4.00 pm	Arrival and registration.	
4.15 pm	Welcome	Murray Edwards, Theatre Manager
4.20 pm	Presentation on the Theatre's strategic plan	Dick Stockford, Board member
4.40 pm	Presentation on the new development	
5.20 pm	BREAK	
5.50 pm	Creative consultation	Facilitated by creativity@work
	First BIG question: How would Wakefield be a worse place if the Theatre did not exist? 60-second soapbox technique Chunking	
	Second BIG question: How can the Theatre's strategic plan be improved? 60-second soapbox Chunking Metaphors – pantomimes	
	Third BIG question: If resources were no object what one thing can you think of that would dramatically improve the Theatre? Flight of fancy – paper aeroplanes creative exercise	
6.55 pm	THANK YOU	Dick Stockford Murray Edwards

Figure 7.1 *Format of an event*

strategic plan as it stood, and any extra ideas the stakeholders could identify. Further creative dimensions were added by inviting each attendee to make their own name badge where they could adopt the name of their favourite actor or character. Each table was also given the name of a Shakespeare play. To provide a further creative dimension, the whole consultation exercise was conducted on the Theatre stage.

GENERATE NEW IDEAS AND ALTERNATIVES FROM THOSE BEING CONSULTED

Brainstorming is not only a useful creativity technique, it also has great potential as a consultation tool. By reframing the whole consultation exercise away from 'What do you think?' to 'What ideas can we generate to improve our situation?' you are transforming the relationship between your stakeholder and the issue you are consulting on. You are also transforming the potential resources available to you for generating new ideas, new insights, and alternative solutions.

Consultative brainstorms open up a new pool of talent of people, who often have far more intimate and relevant experience to the problem than you or your colleagues may have, by bringing a vast range of different age, gender, race, geographical, or socio-economic perspectives to your cause.

OBTAIN VALUABLE MARKET INTELLIGENCE AND INSIGHT

Any problem contains a multitude of questions. An effective consultation session can help identify new issues or dimensions, and highlight questions felt to be more important and significant. One tactic is to use a chunking exercise (see page 99). If many different groups identify a particular question its prevalence would be an indicator of its significance to the target group.

Responses given during the consultation will contain many good ideas or potential ideas. It is essential these are noted and made use of. Far too many consultation exercises generate potential seeds of ideas which are then not acted upon.

Bernard Savage runs marketing consultancy Size 10½ boots. He delivers a service called 'rapport research'. Typically, it is used to engage with hard-to-reach targets. From his experience it is much easier to get in front of a prospective client on the basis of genuinely seeking their views than through a cold-call sales sell. With the face-to-face research and using a structured questionnaire he is able to gain significant insight, as well as rapport and potential goodwill for his client.

Describing his rapport research methodology tool Bernard said:

> A law firm client used the rapport research method to begin a relationship with a senior in-house lawyer for a global automotive company. My client was preparing to launch a major new initiative in the legal marketplace but wanted to fine tune their service offer by commissioning some research.
>
> The goal of employing this research technique was to first build rapport with the prospect. In a convivial meeting rapport was established. We gained valuable insights that helped us later shape the commercial proposition. Having engaged the prospect the next challenge was to build a relationship.
>
> Appealing to the prospect's intrigue in the new service offer, and recognizing people's in-built desire to be consulted, the process yielded valuable insights into what might work at launch and what wouldn't. The prospect valued being asked for his point of view. Put simply, we showed an interest in his company and identified some common ground – in this case an appreciation of the Outer Hebrides!
>
> At the end of the interview the prospect was given the opportunity to learn the outcome of the research and my client's plans for launch in a future meeting and the relationship between my client and the prospect blossomed.

Insight is a very profound tool in creative communications. It can provide a fresh and unexpected perspective. It means you have to think of something that no one has thought of before. Insight requires you look at things differently. For that reason, most of the great sources of 'insight inspiration' are from outside of your immediate world – whether it is your market or product category, or often outside of your geographic marketplace. The creative practitioner has a great role to play in helping to unearth insight through consultation, to provide a starting point for any subsequent creative activity.

 Have you checked if there is scope to obtain further insight on any campaign you are working on?

CREATE SUPER-ADVOCATES FOR YOUR CAUSE

Word-of-mouth (w-o-m) is probably the most powerful communications tool. It is essentially about circulating messages, or memes, relevant to your future success and enabling other people to communicate about you.

W-o-m can however take time for people to engage with other people or allow them to accumulate enough favourable experiences – and subsequently communicate them. Providing opportunities to sample or be involved in a consultation can facilitate your w-o-m buzz.

The w-o-m potential of a situation will be determined by a number of 'contagious attributes'. W-o-m works well when there is a high involvement among customers, where the idea, product, or service has high potential conversation value. Involving targets by consulting with them can create a win-win of getting their views, and sparking them in turn to create very potent viral communications about you, or your product.

KEY LESSONS FOR SUCCESSFUL CREATIVE CONSULTATION

Factors to ensure successful creative consultation activity include the following:

- Early involvement equals better delivery – get involved as soon as possible in plans for any campaign where there is potential for consultation. Brief key players early. Inform them before engaging the community in any wider consultation; their comments can add real impetus and insight into proposed activity, such as a planning application.
- Clear lines of responsibility.
- Clear communications – things can move quickly and with consultation opening up new avenues of contacts a clear process can avoid confusion or messages failing to get through.

111

- Sincerity is crucial – you need to display that you are being genuine in your desire to consult and that you are not going through the motions, or using consultation as a political sop. People really can recognize any serious, honest effort to hear their views and opinions.
- Ensure you have the right audience, either with specific individuals or making your audience at each event as representative as possible. If it is a large event, you can use this to your advantage to demonstrate you are engaging with people like them.
- Make it tangible, literally, by providing items people can touch or feel, or get hold of in some way. Showing people a concept, rather than just telling them about it, invites their participation and engagement, helping people understand it well enough to offer feedback. If you are developing a product or building, prototypes can be critical; people can see and touch the concept and imagine it in use, quickly seeing potential problems and improvements.
- Presenting ideas and information visually helps people grasp what you are saying at a deeper level and engages them in a way that just words cannot do.
- You also need personal listening skills. Any champion of creative consultation has to have a pre-disposition to engaging with people. Simon Hughes, at the UK government's Central Office of Information, is an outstanding practitioner in consultation, with a track record of many innovative impressive events. He is also an example of someone with a passion for listening:

I have always had the ability to talk to anyone and listening came from early experience of working with people. When I was 14, I was chairman of the parish youth committee. I ran the youth club where I came across guys who tried to kick my head in on my way to school who, once you got talking to them, turned out to be really nice people. As a runner I was the only athlete who used to listen to the crowd! I like standing by the door at any event we run and listening to what they are saying to each other – and also learn from their body language.

CHALLENGES WITH CONSULTATION

Creative consultation is a very powerful tool. Effective listening

and recording target audience views can create a very robust process with a very thorough evidence base, providing the information to guard against any negative response.

Yet, the use of creative consultation is often limited in everyday practice. Consulting always takes longer. People seemingly never have time at the beginning of a programme, yet always have more time forced upon them when things either don't work or go wrong. Going ahead without consultation can be false economy.

A key benefit of using consultation is to enhance the sustainability of your campaign; early consultation is likely to identify potential pitfalls to avoid, or secures the buy-in of key audiences.

Sincerity and a genuine commitment to listen and act upon any feedback is crucial for effective consultation. The commissioners of any consultation have to be prepared to take the bad as well as the good news.

Do you give sufficient feedback when engaging with a target group?

FEEDBACK

As with any well-run brainstorming session, following consultation you should always provide feedback to those taking part, ranging from a polite 'thank you' letter to a summary of the findings, or indeed the whole report. Where possible, keep those consulted informed of any subsequent developments.

THE CONSULTATION QUANDARY

Consultation cannot be used all the time. There will inevitably be occasions when decisive action is required. The creative practitioner needs to develop the skills of riding both horses; being open and consultative, coupled with decisive autocratic action on appropriate occasions.

Rather like the apocryphal tale of a former French minister who once said: 'If you want to drain the marsh, don't consult the frogs', sometimes, consultation can get in the way of the optimum added-value solution, or at worst be an excuse for inaction.

Factors leading to when you need to consult or be authoritative are:

- significance and saliency to a target group of a planned change – if it is a low-importance task the best strategy may be to simply get on with it.
- time available;
- degree of urgency;
- need to establish personal and organizational authority.

OVERVIEW

Creative practitioners need to balance their skills in generating different alternatives combined with the need to listen. It is vital that the tools and processes used in facilitating engagement and dialogue do not get in the way of your mission when consulting – to obtain insight, engagement with your target audiences and mutual respect between you.

SUMMARY

1. Creative consultation can enable you to connect directly with target audiences to demonstrate that you are interested in them and are prepared to listen to their concerns.
2. Creative consultation can produce valuable insight, engagement and mutual respect.
3. The benefits of consultation have to be counter-balanced against the need for fast, decisive action.

KEY WORDS FOR YOUR CREATIVITY VOCABULARY

- Insight.
- LISTENING.
- Consultative brainstorms.
- Rapport research.

8

Red Light thinking: the evaluation of ideas

When I was the Social Secretary at university, I had a choice between two young unknown bands; one was to emerge as one of the world's top groups, the Eurythmics, which featured Annie Lennox and Dave Stewart. I chose The Yachts.

A personal experience

Choosing the right idea can be problematic. For many creative practitioners, the non-sexy part of a brainstorming session is the evaluation stage. This is perhaps the most critical part, where the potential to develop new insights and ideas should be harnessed or else a potential gem is lost. Practitioners tend to use the brainstorm as an end in itself, and immediately run with one or two of the ideas emerging from the session. This is why it is important to recognize the distinctions between Green Light and Red Light thinking.

The first stage, Green Light thinking, is based on creation, being uninhibited in thought and stressing the positive. The second

stage, Red Light thinking, emphasizes judgement, reason, evaluation, and where things may or may not work.

Underlying the use of Red Light thinking must be a commitment to derive the optimum added value. Unlike Green Light thinking, this determination is not reflected in an 'anything goes' approach. It focuses instead on what makes an idea viable, robust from potential criticism, and able to survive in order to do justice to the quality of the original idea.

FORMAL EVALUATION METHODS

For any technique that generates ideas, it is essential to establish at the outset a screening for the end product. Otherwise, there is a tendency to be highly subjective and to look at what is written down and say: 'I like that, I don't like that...'.

Most techniques for evaluation consist either of a screening process, or a sequence to follow for putting an idea into action, and usually a combination of the two.

Screening processes

Ideally, Green Light thinking will have been used to generate as many ideas as possible. It is essential to find a way of rapidly selecting viable options, without throwing out the potential gems of truly creative ideas.

You can screen ideas quickly in several ways. Although these do not entirely avoid subjectivity, they will help assessment to be reasonably unbiased. The first task is to weed out some of the ideas, so that the rest are manageable and time and energy can be concentrated on those with most potential.

Screening method 1

A simple screening process could consist of the following questions:

- Is the idea compatible with the brand values?
- Is the idea compatible with the public relations objectives and strategy?
- Is it legal?

- Can it be developed within a realistic budget and timescales?
- Is it likely to provide added value?
- Are the commitments and risks acceptable?

Alternatively, using your intuitive judgement, you could make a gut-feeling check against your own particular criteria: does the idea have novelty or has it been used before; is it attractive or relevant; and is it feasible to get the idea off the ground?

Only after this preliminary screening should you examine the ideas further. This quickly filters out the really bad ideas and the no-hopers.

Screening method 2

A second screening method is to categorize the ideas into groups with a common theme or element. For example, the screening could be based on the following three broad categories:

1. Realistic ideas or themes that can be put into action immediately.
2. Intriguing ideas that are still embryonic but that have potential as a starting point for thinking about at a later stage.
3. No-hopers.

This clustering of large numbers of ideas can make it easier to make choices between groups as opposed to selecting individual ideas. It helps you to think more strategically about the ideas as a whole. Grouping them together helps prevent the instant urge to accept or reject specific individual ideas.

Second-stage screening

More detailed screening is possible. Rate the ideas against a specific range of objectives, such as their ability to promote a certain message, or their ability to link up with another specific promotion. The criteria should be divided between 'Essential' and 'Desirable' objectives, and any idea that fails the 'Essential' criterion should be eliminated immediately.

Rather than a straightforward Yes/No evaluation, rate the elements 1–10 under 'Essential' and 'Desirable'. An additional weighting can be introduced to signify the relative importance of different objectives used in the criteria. So, if one criterion was thought to be twice as important as another, any rating given to it

would be multiplied by two. From these figures, it is possible to to establish a scoring system for the ideas and come up with a solution based on the highest score.

Although this may sound objective, there is still a tendency for people to manipulate the figures to arrive mysteriously at their preferred subjective choice. Alternatively, you could use a formal voting system, as with Nominal Group Technique.

Putting an idea into action

The next step is to consider how you will put the idea into action. A useful technique is a form of critical path analysis, where you seek to identify what could go wrong, examine the key causes of potential failures, and identify any preventive action that may be required. This is particularly necessary for the illustration stage of the creative process, where practitioners give insufficient thought to how to sell their ideas.

Avoid the soft 'consensus' solution

There is a tendency in decision making, particularly in groups, to agree to a compromise solution to avoid conflict or upsetting group harmony. This is known in management jargon as the 'Abilene Paradox', or, in an anglicized form, the 'Basingstoke Paradox', so-called in each case after a typically nondescript provincial town. (The paradox is that, apparently, a family once visited the town – even though no one in the group really wanted to – because everyone thought it was the choice of the others. It is similar to the phrase 'a camel is a horse designed by a committee'.)

The only real safeguard against group consensus dominating an evaluation is for one or more in the group to be committed to the outcome of the creative activity. If everyone concerned is looking at the decision-making process as an end in itself – rather than trying to generate the best added-value option – the likelihood is that a compromise, suboptimal solution will emerge.

 Look back on any creative failures that you have been involved with and consider whether or not compromises in the evaluation stage affected the outcome.

BENJAMIN FRANKLIN'S 'PRUDENTIAL ALGEBRA' TECHNIQUE

One of the great minds of America, Benjamin Franklin, when faced with having to make decisions, developed a technique that he called 'moral' or 'prudential algebra'. He divided a sheet of paper into two columns, with the word 'Pro' at the head of one column and the word 'Con' heading the other. As given by Dale Carnegie in his *How to Stop Worrying and Start Living* (Carnegie, 1952), Franklin described his technique thus:

> During three or four days' consideration, I put down under the different heads short hints of the different motives that at different times occur to me, for or against the measure. I endeavour to estimate their respective weights; and where I find two (one on each side) that seem equal, I strike them both out.
>
> If I find a reason 'Pro' equal to some two reasons 'Con' I strike out the three... Thus proceeding, I find at length where the balance lies; if after a day or two of further consideration, nothing new that is of importance occurs on either side, I come to a determination accordingly... I have found great advantage from this kind of equation.

Franklin thus describes how he used the incubation stage effectively in the creative process, when he took three or four days' deliberation. Franklin's scientific terms of equation may appear quite rational, and yet the real value of the technique is in articulating inner instincts on a subject. Rather than being entirely objective, the method encourages you to write down more extensive or detailed points in either of the 'Pros' or 'Cons' columns, depending on how you instinctively feel about the problem you are facing. Consequently, the end decision is not so much a calculation as an articulation of your intuition and how you feel deep down about a question (see Chapter 13 – Take your hunches to lunch).

EXTERNAL EVALUATION

Deciding what ideas to run with can be difficult, in spite of any number of sophisticated screening techniques. An easy way of finalizing your choice of different creative options is simply to ask someone who is not connected with the work what they think. The closer they are to the target audience you want to reach, the better.

Informal external contacts

The computer industry has the problem of moving in a rapidly dynamic market; as soon as a product is launched, there is the risk that it will be overtaken by other developments in the industry. One tactic is to develop new products – not just in the laboratory, but working closely with what are called 'beta test site' customers. These forward-looking customers are leading users of products, usually at the cutting edge of innovation and at the forefront of developing new ways of doing things. By putting new products on live trial in the marketplace at the earliest opportunity, the computer companies are able to identify quickly not just problems that may emerge through technical hitches but also new opportunities, perhaps finding new uses of the product beyond those initially envisaged.

You might experience this type of chain reaction when you present a new idea. The client or manager may say: 'That's a good idea because we could use it for this problem.' You hastily agree, as if it was an obvious extension of your original idea. With this in mind, I frequently run embryonic ideas past journalists with whom I have an established relationship and ask: 'Do you think this idea would work?'

One of the key figures to influence British advertising is the humble office cleaner. A number of times I have witnessed a hard-working creative slaving away, late at the office, unsure which particular treatment of an advertisement works best. The appearance of the cleaner provides an excellent opportunity to obtain feedback on how the person on the street would react to a particular idea.

 Consider your informal contacts with colleagues in other departments or among your clients. Is there anyone you can develop a 'beta test site' relationship with, where you can say: 'Can I run this idea past you?' or 'Do you think this could work?'

Chapter 13 will look at ways in which the creative practitioner can use role models for evaluation. They provide detachment and greater objectivity, answering the question: 'What is the likely reaction to this idea?'

Formal external groups

The use of focus groups, or panels, to consider new ideas is a well-established technique in qualitative market research. A group representing a sample of the target audience can be used, either as a one-off trial or for regular tracking. New ideas can be formally run past the group so as to gain the members' reaction, and potential acceptance or rejection can be assessed. The group's views are monitored and can be interpreted by a professional researcher.

For many public relations campaigns, there may not be sufficient budget or time to run a formal focus group. Nonetheless, with some creative thought, the idea can be adapted. I have run informal research sessions among groups as diverse as the homeless (for an environmental company, to gauge their likely involvement in a recycling scheme) and stockbrokers (for identifying key messages for the launch of a new financial product). Often, all that is required is: 'Can I have a few minutes of your time to research...?' or 'Can I have your advice on...?'

YOU DECIDE

The techniques centring on Red Light thinking that are described in this book are useful for sifting material and helping to avoid killing off potentially good ideas at birth. They also assist in providing a focus for evaluation and further investigation. Yet, no matter how thorough an evaluation is, the decision to run with a particular idea will rest with someone – possibly you.

Professor Morris Stein, one of the world's leading experts on creativity, once asked me: 'When do abstract artists know when their painting is finished?' My answer to this question is the same as to the one posed in our industry when evaluating our ideas. As long as you do not let an ego get in the way – whether you are an abstract painter or a public relations practitioner – you must have a personal belief, based upon your confidence and the development of your professional skills, that what you have produced is right; that the creative product is ready to go, and that it is fit for its purpose. The creative product that bears your signature must not compromise your reputation.

SUMMARY

1. Red Light thinking is the most critical part of the creative function. Potential gems of ideas may be lost if an evaluation is not done properly.
2. Screening techniques are available to sift and evaluate ideas.
3. External contacts – ranging from asking the office cleaner's opinion, to formal focus groups – can help evaluate ideas.
4. All techniques for evaluating ideas are still subjective. The ultimate decision is down to someone – possibly you.
5. Basingstoke is a dull place to visit.

KEY WORDS FOR YOUR CREATIVITY VOCABULARY

- External contacts.
- Intuition.
- Screening.

9

Creativity is not just for photocalls

Well, the first thing I would do is cut the grass outside your offices.
Response of the late Robert Davy, when asked by a lawnmower company
how he would improve its public relations

Most practitioners fall into the trap of perceiving creativity as a tactical tool, to be used in activities such as coming up with ideas for photocalls, new angles for a story, or as an element in the design of promotional material. Yet the creative function is inherently a strategic as well as a tactical tool.

CREATIVITY AS A STRATEGIC TOOL

Strategy is one of those concepts that is in danger of becoming an end in itself. 'What we need is a strategy document on this', was one call to inaction remembered from my days in local government. However, it is much more than this. Put at its simplest, strategy has been neatly defined by Graham Lancaster of Biss Lancaster as 'the shortest line between two points, identifying

where you are, and where you want to be'. (Another alternative definition uses the analogy of seeking to be inebriated: the objective is to get drunk, the strategy is to go to the pub, and the tactics are to have 10 pints!)

The creative practitioner can use creativity both to establish and to review an organization's vision of where it sees itself and where it is going. To Steve Gebbett of Charles Barker:

> The way creativity feeds into strategy is at the 'big picture' end. In some respects creativity is a way of challenging an existing strategy with ideas that may have an effect on the direction of the main strategic thrust of the organization. The new ideas in themselves may also have strategic legs to give further dimensions to the organization's activities.

The creative function can be used in all aspects of devising, identifying and articulating the strategy, particularly in two key areas: strategy as a statement of intent, and in its everyday performance as a direction indicator for values and behaviour within an organization.

Strategy as an indicator of organizational value and behaviour

An organization, even with a clearly articulated strategy, does not exist in a vacuum in its quest to get from A to B in the shortest space of time. If it is to be successful in its journey, it must also match its intent with the necessary supporting values and behaviours.

Alan Preece of the University of East Anglia said when interviewed: 'Creativity as a strategic tool exists as one of the values of the organization. If an organization can say explicitly that it is creative, then that is one of its values that it must then prove, by the way it treats people and the way it treats creativity.' This point about creativity being a strategic behaviour is, as Graham Lancaster believes, an absolutely crucial element in the functioning of successful organizations:

> I actually think creativity comes out of planning and strategic thinking. Eighty per cent of creativity is understanding the business issue, the customer, and the market dynamics. When I think about the successful organizations... [they live] the strategy. They know

their business, they know their customers, they know their business goal and, because they are steeped in that, they are able through PR, advertising, merchandizing or design to *behaviourally* demonstrate their creativity.

Strategy maps

A technique to ensure that strategic statements are counterbalanced with supporting behaviours is to draw what is known as a 'strategy map'.

At the top of a sheet of paper, put your organization's philosophy and mission, followed by its business objectives. Beneath this detail the various processes and behaviours that are required to deliver, day in and day out, the statement of intent. The result is a hierarchy of the strategy, with its articulation as a vision at the top and as guidance for everyday actions at the bottom. Table 9.1 shows the one used by GREEN communications.

CREATIVITY AS A TACTICAL TOOL: 24 PRACTICAL EXAMPLES

This book is intended to fill a void in the information on creativity in public relations. Rather than include a series of examples of outstanding individual campaigns – which are already well documented in the reviews of award-winning programmes – a number of 'soundbites' of creative public relations practice are instead set out on pages 125–38. These have in some way contributed added value to the tactics of achieving their task, and they demonstrate how creativity can be applied to any aspect of public relations practice.

Creativity with photocalls

Generating maximum impact and media interest in a press launch can be a major challenge for practitioners. When Steve Gebbett of Charles Barker sought to launch a chocolate bar for Cadbury, he used a combination of old and new technology to stunning effect. An image of the chocolate brand, Wispa Gold, was projected by laser on to the dome of St Paul's cathedral, resulting in a very unusual and dramatic photo – and extensive media coverage. Wispa Gold sold out within days.

Table 9.1 *An example of a strategy map*

Company philosophy (vision)	Our vision is to make a difference to the life of our customers by expanding their life, personality and story to their key audiences, or extend their creative abilities in some way.
	We seek to use our professional abilities to the best advantage of our clients, share our knowledge, skills and insights, and throw in the wish to inspire, laugh, and learn from each other.
	We are second to none.
Mission statement	We use our philosophy to meet the needs of our existing clients and attract new clients.
Objectives	To retain existing clients.
	To grow the company in the year ahead by 10 per cent in sales through new clients and client growth.
	To retain valued staff.
Behaviours	Every action should comply with: 'Would a "consultancy second to none" do this?'
	Schedule weekly/quarterly creative reviews. Six-monthly appraisals for staff.
	Every week, pose the question: 'What extra can we do for our clients?'
	Always be honest with clients.

Creativity through identifying allies

In any campaign, creativity can be used to identify potential allies for your particular cause. When the Leeds Development Corporation (LDC) was facing the formal wind-up of its activities in April 1995, there was a widespread view within the organization that Leeds City Council, which had vigorously opposed the existence of the Corporation, would come in and remove the LDC's billboards that proclaimed the successes of its work. By posing to myself the question 'Who would Leeds City Council *not* pick a fight with?', I came up with the answer: God.

A restoration appeal by Leeds Parish Church was chosen as a suitable link. The LDC signs were given over to the Church's appeal for a peppercorn rent, and were redesigned with a message supporting the appeal, but still including a reference to Leeds Development Corporation. Several years later they were still standing.

Creativity in corporate hospitality

Rather than pay expensive prices for tickets for hospitality packages at major events such as Twickenham, the Yorkshire Building Society sponsors a local Rugby Union team. Part of the deal, devised by David Holmes, the Society's Communications Manager, is for the Society to receive tickets from the local rugby club for internationals at Twickenham. As a consequence, the local rugby club is able to generate additional funding (from matching sponsorship, which doubles the amount they receive from the Society). The net result is tickets at a lower price than from hospitality packages, a very worthwhile local community sponsorship with attendant publicity, and additional help for a local club.

Creativity in the use of media

Looking at unusual channels of communication can add value to a campaign, and I owe my start in public relations to this. At university I stood for election to a student union post. Each candidate was allowed the cost of several thousand leaflets and posters. However, soon into the campaign I realized that my message was not getting through as all the candidates were leaving the manifesto leaflets in the same place in the student union refectory. I thought about ways in which it would be possible to get two or three minutes of undivided attention from the students to read my manifesto and make me stand out from the other candidates. The answer was to stick the manifestos on the back of toilet doors. As a result, I won – and the rest, as they say, is history.

Creativity in boring appointment stories

Every partner who joins north-west England law firm Davies Wallis Foyster does not have a run-of-the-mill head-and-shoulders photo to accompany the announcement of his or her appointment.

Instead, the firm goes to great lengths to create a photo that portrays some aspect of the new partner's personality, interest or work – or, indeed, some combination of these three. The photos are generally outstanding in their own right, but in addition the practice's Public Relations Manager, Dawn Boswell, then creatively seeks out unusual outlets for them.

On one occasion a partner with an interest in horse racing had his photo taken wearing a jaunty titfer and holding both his winnings and a copy of the *Sporting Life*. By including the racing newspaper on her distribution list, Dawn generated additional coverage, which also led to the partner picking up new client contacts and goodwill, and extra business was generated as a result of the article.

Creativity with an anniversary

Look beyond the routine in celebrating an anniversary. For Trinity and Burton Arcades – one of the smallest shopping centres in Leeds – considerable added value was achieved in celebrating its 25th anniversary in 1998 by identifying a topical opportunity.

The year the centre opened, 1973, was the year Leeds United were beaten by underdogs Sunderland in the FA Cup Final. The game was memorable for an outstanding display by Sunderland goalkeeper Jim Montgomery, who kept the mighty Leeds team at bay. In 1998 a charity penalty shoot-out competition was arranged at the shopping centre with veteran players Jim Montgomery and Leeds United's Norman Hunter taking part, and an invitation was issued to United fans to avenge their defeat. Considerable media coverage was obtained as a result of what was potentially a mundane anniversary opportunity.

Creative use of a negative opportunity

When public relations entrepreneur Max Clifford was faced with a potentially negative media enquiry from the *Sun* newspaper about his client, comedian Freddie Starr, he creatively harnessed the opportunity, leading to one of the most memorable tabloid front pages of all time.

Faced with the unusual claim that Mr Starr had been cruel to a friend's pet hamster, instead of trying to suppress or deny the story, a deal was struck with the paper. Max Clifford recalled: 'I

have seen Freddie put very strange things in his mouth over the years, but never a hamster, I have to say. Freddie wanted me to try and stop it, but my decision was to go with it.' Consequently, the *Sun*'s front page ran with the memorable headline: 'Freddie Starr ate my hamster'.

Max added: 'The arrangement I made was for the *Sun* to do a piece the following day with Freddie and a pet hamster called "Sandwich", with Freddie saying that he would never eat his sandwich. He was about to do a British tour. As a result of the coverage, the tour was totally sold out and Freddie made references to the hamster as part of his act. Years later most people still remember it.'

Creativity by improving a news release without altering a word on it

It is possible to make a news release more creative without even altering a single word. Think 'outside the box' (see Chapter 13) and recognize that the release does not just consist of words but also of the paper it is written on. Why not change the format of the paper – or even make the release smell. For example, if you are running an anti-smoking campaign, you can make the news release stink of tobacco smoke to highlight one of the negatives of cigarettes.

My own consultancy extends the characteristics of a press release by attaching to it what we call a 'Quality card'. The reply-paid card offers to pay £5 to a journalists' union charity if the attached release is deemed by target journalists to be badly written.

So, do not assume that a press release is just set text. Be creative in extending its features and functions.

Creative opportunities in parliamentary lobbying

The 75th anniversary of the Scouting movement back in 1981 was given outstanding publicity by linking up with parliamentarians. Douglas Smith, now of Westminster Advisers, persuaded the then Speaker of the House of Commons, the late George Thomas – himself a former Scout – to invite 74 other Scouts, former and

129

current, to Speaker's House for a reception there, and later on to the terrace at the Houses of Parliament.

The guests were carefully selected to include famous politicians (Harold Wilson, Geoffrey Howe) sportsmen (Stirling Moss), stage and screen stars (Derek Nimmo, Leonard Rossiter and Roy Kinnear), and a range of active young Scouters from across the country, embracing every television region. Structuring the event in this way enabled good advance coverage, with interviews with the youngsters on receiving their invitations, and also national press and media coverage on the day.

The actors taking part also rolled up their trouser legs and put on Cub caps for the photocall. Added interest was obtained by involving Arthur Primmer, who had been at Baden Powell's Scout camp on Brownsea Island. He attended the event, aged 93, and his picture with a 7-year-old Cub Scout also made the front pages. Every year since, the current Speaker of the House of Commons has hosted a Scouts event at the House.

Creativity in selecting a winner for an award

Award schemes are often used to promote a particular issue. A number use the technique of selecting a winner who is topical and will therefore provide added value in news coverage.

I was once faced, in my role as a member of an awards committee, with a major problem. Just two weeks before the awards ceremony, we were let down by a prospective recipient. It would have been embarrassing to approach anyone of note at such short notice. The solution was to creatively redefine the potential targets, and come up with the idea of giving it to a celebrity who had recently died, partly on the premise that they were not in a position to turn it down!

Creatively identifying and campaigning on an issue

When superstore chain Asda wanted to match its behaviour with values of a different kind in offering good value shopping for working people and their families, it creatively identified a potential campaign. It sought to change the law to scrap the Net Book Agreement (NBA), which was dictating at what price books could

be sold in the UK. Although legal challenges had been mounted previously by small booksellers, Asda was able to bring considerable clout to its efforts, which saw the abolition of the NBA and considerable publicity highlighting Asda's positioning on good value shopping.

Creativity with a 'Note to News Editor'

Every part of a news release has the potential for creativity to provide added value, even the footnote of 'Note to News Editors'.

When staging a press conference for Yorkshire Water Authority announcing the launch of a new sewerage scheme for Leeds, various creative proposals for the event had been rejected by the Authority management, resulting in a potentially boring story. Adding an innocuous sentence, namely 'Journalists are advised to have a light breakfast before attending the press conference', to the invitation provided an irresistible challenge to local news editors. They sent their reporters along eager to see stomach-churning sewage works. This resulted in extensive additional coverage.

Creativity in journalists' entertainment

Maintaining personal contacts with journalists is increasingly difficult. The media employ fewer journalists and use technology such as 'faxwalling' – where practitioners are fobbed off with the request to fax their story through – to make it harder to establish personal contact.

This is particularly difficult in intensely competitive sectors, such as personal finance, with many financial institutions competing for the attention of just a few journalists. One creative trick, used by a leading practitioner, is to book a table at the most fashionable restaurant. This is then used as the bait to interest the journalist for lunch, rather than trying to arrange a meeting and then seek a restaurant.

Creative packaging of an element of the service or product

When Yorkshire Water Authority wanted to launch a local plumbing service in the region, a potentially routine affair was

given dramatic added value by packaging one element of the story. The Authority's four-week training course included a day's training on customer service. This element was repackaged as a 'Charm School for Plumbers', and a passing-out parade was arranged to mark the graduation of these plumbers. Worldwide media coverage was obtained directly as a result of the added value from this repackaging of one part of the product or service.

Creatively spotting opportunities in the detail of a situation

Drawing attention to one detail of an issue or story, it is possible to create considerable added value in news opportunities.

When producing a historical leaflet guide for my home village of Crofton, just outside Wakefield, Yorkshire, one unusual feature was the village's chip shop. It suffered from mining subsidence, which had caused the building to tilt slightly to one side. This was identified as the lead news angle, with the press release intro reading: 'A former mining village which boasts a leaning chip shop is aiming to put itself on the tourist map...'. The release also contained the quote: 'The Italians have their leaning tower, we've got our chip ship.' Coverage was obtained in national media and television about the 'Leaning Chip Shop of Crofton'. Considerable added value was obtained for a story of a photocopied leaflet about an inconspicuous village.

Creativity for a launch party

Creativity in selecting the right venue for a launch event can be crucial in ensuring that the event is memorable. However, the tendency is to consider mainstream or established venues, and this may not always be the most effective approach.

When creative practitioner Mark Borkowski sought a venue for launching a promotion for the Action Man children's toy, he used a multi-storey car park. By suitably dressing the location up, he created a unique location for a media launch party.

Creative use of a personal name

When Walkers Crisps wanted to launch an improved flavour to their salt 'n' vinegar crisps, Hill and Knowlton obtained added

value in the promotion by devising a new name for the product. They creatively linked the product with the crisp manufacturer's well-established promotional campaign with former England footballer, Gary Lineker. By coming up with the new name, 'Salt 'n' Lineker', they generated considerable additional consumer interest and publicity opportunities.

Creative use of spokespersons

The choice of spokesperson for a campaign can provide added value to the communication. What if none is available? This was the challenge when Leeds-based Treats Ice Cream undertook a campaign to encourage a management buy-out of the company. None of the managers could publicly speak out against the then parent company. The solution was to use the media itself as the spokesperson.

The *Yorkshire Evening Post* in Leeds was taken into confidence and the situation explained about how the managers were effectively gagged. The newspaper supported the campaign's key objective: to save the future of the company for its 350-strong workforce. The *Yorkshire Evening Post* mounted an outstanding campaign against the closure. Rather than using a spokesperson from the company, the paper directly asked the questions about the parent company's motives for closures.

Creativity in the 'worst day of the year'

How do you make a creative idea for generating media coverage for a travel company really stand out? One idea is to give your idea some form of legitimacy and technical validity. The Porter Novelli consultancy came up with the idea of an academic officially defining the 'worst day of the year' which appropriately arose during the time its client Sky Travel wanted to raise its profile for holiday bookings.

The consultancy approached Dr Cliff Arnall, an academic at Cardiff University who specializes in seasonal disorders, who devised a mathematical equation for defining the worst day of the year:

$$\frac{[W + (D - d)] \times T^Q}{M \times N_A}$$

The model is broken down using six immediately identifiable factors; weather (W), amount of financial debt due to spending over Christmas and the New Year period (D), amount of next pay cheque (d), time since Christmas (T), time since failing our new year's resolutions (Q), low motivational levels (M) and the feeling of a need to take action (N_A). The equation calculated that in 2005, Monday 24 January was 'officially' the worst day of the year.

The idea generated strong added value clearly linking the news interest of the worst day of the year and the business objectives of clients booking holidays (ideally with Sky Travel.) No one had ever before confirmed, through maths or science, the existence of 'January blues', let alone defined the worst day for those blues. It was a simple idea that everyone could grasp and created debate – was it or wasn't it the worst day of the year?

The idea possessed credible logic – the weather, personal debts, failure to maintain a New Year's resolution, etc, do all contribute to mood. As it was a defined day the media had a focus, exploiting a traditionally quiet news day. The campaign fulfilled its objectives of creating a voice for Sky Travel during this key booking time and raising the company's profile above its competitors.

Creativity from someone else's creative idea of the 'worst day of the year'

Just because someone else comes up with an idea it does not mean you cannot capitalize on it. Porter Novelli's idea of 'the worst day of the year' also provided a piggy-back opportunity for my creativity consultancy creativity@work; I quickly responded with a further news story response using the angle 'you can avoid being depressed on this day by being creative', and obtained extensive coverage.

Noting the prospects for repeating the idea for 2006 I was amazed to find the idea was not being repeated. Recognizing its further potential, I obtained the blessing from the London consultancy and Dr Arnall to reuse their original concept.

I did however recognize that new twists and additional new dimensions were needed to get full value from reusing the idea. Fresh impetus was achieved through branding the day by elevating the significance of the occasion from just a date in the calendar to a special themed event with the brand 'Beat Blue

Monday', transforming it from a one-off news story into an annual institution.

Various 'Blue Monday' web domains were already taken up by links to the band New Order (with their song of the same name) and organizations ranging from escort agencies to recruitment firms. However, the domain name www.beatbluemonday.org.uk was available and also better served the idea of overcoming depression.

The theme of the day was defined as 'circumstances may conspire to create the potential for 23 January (which was the third Monday in the month for 2006) to be the most depressing day of the year – but you can choose to overcome these problems, with our help.'

A charity link was established to provide legitimacy and also create a positive spin-off from the media coverage. The Samaritans was identified as an ideal partner: the organization helps people 24/7 address the challenges of being depressed. In fact the timing was significant; this period sadly is the peak period for suicide attempts.

The Art of Propaganda Gallery at the Wakefield Media Centre was adapted into a 'Happiness Centre' where anyone could come in and have their mood transformed by happy images and the chance to blow bubbles.

Creative news angles were featured in a press pack created providing different news angles and tips on 'how to overcome the most depressing day'. Creative links were created, from a leading chain of health and fitness centres through to comedian Danny Wallace, who has set up his own 'Karma Army' dedicated to doing random acts of kindness. (Danny had previously exhibited at the Art of Propaganda gallery.)

The campaign secured extensive worldwide coverage by capitalizing on recycling someone else's idea to raise profile of the Samaritans and the Wakefield Media Centre. Plus, it succeeded in turning the most depressing day of the year into a commercial opportunity.

The only downside was that the day coincided with my eldest daughter's birthday which prompted her comment: 'Thanks, Dad, for formally confirming my birthday as the most depressing day of the year!'

Creativity to make a mailing more memorable

One of the most tedious aspects of media relations work is to follow up a mailing to check whether or not it has been received, and if there is a need to further 'sell in' the story to the journalist. The first hurdle in this process is making a routine news release stand out in some way.

For a hotel client based in Kendal in the English Lake District, a small piece of Kendal mint cake was attached to the news release as a way of adding distinction to the new season's launch mailing. When journalist follow-up calls were made, the first hurdle of whether they recalled receiving the release was made easier by adding the detail: 'It was the release that had the Kendal mint cake attached to it.' As a result, awareness was virtually 100 per cent among targeted journalists.

Care should be taken, however, to ensure that any creative addition to the mailing is not misinterpreted as trying to bribe or induce the journalist to use the story beyond its journalistic considerations. A financial PR campaign that included giving expensive computerized personal organizers to journalists was seen by many as overstepping the mark.

Creative use of gambling as an 'insurance'

A new twist to providing a payback to publicity was provided by public relations consultancy Communique, in a promotional stunt for its brewery client Boddingtons. When the England cricket team seemed to be facing yet another humiliation against the touring Australians, the consultancy identified a potential opportunity. Paul Carroll describes the situation thus:

> We got one of the Boddingtons models to visit the England team on training day to present bottles of Boddingtons and tell the team to have a bit more 'bottle' and to cream the Aussies. To give a further angle to the story, we said that we would also put a £1,000 bet on England to win, so confident were we of the inspirational powers of Boddingtons. Brilliant idea we thought. We did good shots, everything we could have done, but no newspapers touched it.
>
> Just as we thought we had a disaster on our hands, England surprisingly won the Test and we won £5,000 on the bet. The client thought that it was PR paying for itself. By the time we deducted the expenses of the photography and all the other stuff, we had £3,000

extra in the PR budget. Who said PR can't pay its own way? Maybe we should put all our clients' money on horses and dogs!

Creative use of an unusual event

How does a niche brand stand out against global brands with big budgets to match? Major alcohol brands already dominate music, comedy and sport. Instead of getting lost in brand soup or relying on expensive sponsorship deals, Cow, Hoegaarden's PR agency in the UK created its own event – 'Urban Oasis'.

A 'natural pub' created entirely out of grass appeared overnight at two locations in the heart of London and Manchester. This was intended to be the physical embodiment of 'Urban Oasis', an escape from the concrete jungle complete with grass tables and chairs and a 'natural' jukebox playing birdsong and other sounds from nature.

Cow worked with The Office of Subversive Architects, an art collective well known for challenging public opinion on environment and its impact on people's state of mind, to make the installation credible with the media and art world, and to prompt further debate and coverage.

The installations became a haven for would-be Hoegaarden drinkers during the summer with people using the space to relax and unwind at lunchtime and after work. Cow brought the installations to life for a wider audience via guerrilla-marketing tactics including living turf patches, grass billboards, and pavement chalkings. The campaign achieved an OTS of 77 million, an estimated 30,000 people visited the installations, and most importantly, 48,000 glasses of Hoegaarden were consumed!

Creativity in event sponsorship

Creative sponsorship can breathe new life into even the most well-established of products. Frank PR identified a new opportunity for the 107-year-old condiment, HP Sauce with the sport of snooker. Following negotiations with the organizers of the Masters Snooker Tournament, televised live by the BBC, HP Sauce became the 'Official Sponsor of the Brown Ball', the first time anyone had ever sponsored a ball in the sport.

To commemorate the deal, Frank persuaded legendary snooker player Jimmy White to change his name by deed poll to Jimmy

Brown (who got so engaged with the idea he actually even preferred his new name of 'James Brown'!).

The publicity surrounding the announcement of the sponsorship, Jimmy Brown's successful progress in the tournament, the controversy it provoked within sporting and marketing circles, combined with the sheer cheek of it all, meant the campaign generated in excess of £3.5 million pounds' worth of editorial coverage in a week and won a host of marketing awards. Jimmy lost in the semi-final of the tournament. Perhaps ironically he missed the brown ball and his opponent then made the break that won the match.

 Look back on your career. What work sticks in your mind as particularly creative? Reflect on what added value was achieved and how the idea was generated. Are there any lessons to be learned?

SUMMARY

1. Creativity is a strategic as well as a tactical tool.
2. Creativity is itself a strategic value and behaviour.
3. Creativity can be used in any situation to provide added value.
4. You are likely to have at least one better example of creative public relations from your own work or study than the examples used in this chapter.

KEY WORDS FOR YOUR CREATIVITY VOCABULARY

- Positioning.
- Strategy map.

10

Obstacles to creativity

A very sad experience in my life highlighted the difficulties we sometimes face in attempting to channel our thoughts and purposes on a specific task of being creative and coming up with new ideas.

One of my very best friends, Amanda, died from breast cancer at the age of 34. It was probably the most traumatic experience of my life. Although her illness was long evident, the impact of her death really shook me. Sitting at my office desk some three days later, I was unable to focus on anything, least of all work. Morose, I became energized by thinking that I would write down all my thoughts and feelings about Amanda and give them to her husband Dave.

My hand began to write, and out flowed what I wanted to be the most fulsome description of my emotions, memories and feelings. This was probably the most intense act of my life – I was focusing all my thoughts on the single act of pouring out these feelings.

And yet, within minutes, completely random and different thoughts seemed to race across my mind, cutting across my thoughts of Amanda. After a number of these uninvited mental

intrusions, I turned on myself angrily, saying: 'For goodness sake! Here you are dealing with the biggest tragedy you have ever personally known, and you are letting your mind wander off. Stop letting these unconnected thoughts take your focus off your feelings about Amanda.'

Later, reflecting on this experience, I concluded that the mind is rather like a wild animal. It will, after a short period, resist being penned in, having its energies channelled against its will. My experience appears to be echoed by some of the great minds, such as the inventor Thomas Edison who remarked: 'There is no expedient to which a man will not resort to avoid the labour of thinking', while the writer Ralph Waldo Emerson observed: 'Thinking is the hardest task in the world.' As Steve Gebbett of Charles Barker reflected in an interview for this book: 'Creativity, in computer terms, does use this huge amount of RAM, and I wouldn't encourage any creative meeting lasting, frankly, much longer than 40 minutes.'

Looking at why people tend to shy away from having to think up new ideas, it is clear that the inherently difficult task of concentrating our individual thoughts and energies on a specific subject runs contrary to the intrinsic character of the mind. It is inclined to want to deal with several different tasks simultaneously, or in quick succession, rather than concentrating on one specific thought for a prolonged period.

In light of this, it's worth looking at the blocks to creativity, such as that uncomfortable feeling in the brain, in order to understand them and use appropriate tactics to overcome them.

THE NATURE OF THE PROBLEM

You don't need more creative solutions, you need more creative questions.

Comment to a client

The nature of the problem could be a major obstacle to creative thinking. Any problem will fit somewhere within the parameters of either a 'well-defined' problem or an 'ill-structured' problem. By identifying the nature of the problem itself, practitioners can assess the task they are facing and where they need to concentrate their efforts to achieve an added value solution.

An ill-structured problem can be defined as one that involves a new challenge for which you have had no previous experience, knowledge or understanding, and for which you consequently have no ready solution at hand to call upon and apply. Such problems are the product of some aspect of novelty, complexity, or ambiguity in a situation. What sets an ill-defined problem apart from a well-defined one is that the former requires problem solvers to contribute to the problem definition – remember that in the information stage of the creative process the formulation of the problem is identified as a key creative task.

There can be a tendency for practitioners to seek solutions before the problem is properly understood. They focus their efforts on creating solutions, such as ideas for campaigns, without really diagnosing the fundamental root cause or issue of the problem. As a result, there can be the frustration of either not being able to come up with a creative solution or the ideas themselves being evidently superficial or off-target.

The example given in Chapter 1 showed how the launch of alcopop drinks posed the problem of a new product in a new market, where there were no clear structures and guidelines on what was, and what was not, permissible. Similarly, practitioners dealing with public affairs questions for their organizations are faced with numerous ill-structured issues. In order to manage the reputation of their organizations, the public relations staff need to identify where they stand and how they will react to these.

The complexity of a task, or what can be called 'the fog of the detail', may in itself present an obstacle to generating a creative solution. Through not being able to establish the big picture, or an overview or context of the situation, the practitioner can be prevented from identifying the real cause of a problem, or may even be found to be defining the problem too narrowly.

Ultimately, this will determine the paradigm of how you define the task and subsequently frame any creative activity.

 Look back to any task you have recently been given. Ask yourself how well you defined the problem. Could you have been more specific, or even broadened the brief?

POOR GREEN LIGHT/RED LIGHT THINKING IN THE CREATIVE PROCESS

Never trust a chauffeur who hasn't passed a driving test.
Observation to training course delegates

Two modes of thinking were identified in Chapter 2, namely Green Light and Red Light thinking, and Chapter 4 showed how ideas evolve through the creative process. By using this knowledge, it is possible not only to make the most of your creativity, but also to avoid the negative obstacles.

Poor Green Light thinking skills

To achieve results using Green Light thinking requires a set of supporting skills and abilities at both a personal and organizational level. Potential problems include the following:

- *Overcoming the fear of looking foolish.* As Tom Watson, founder of IBM, once observed: 'The way to accelerate your success is to double your failure rate.' Failure is a necessary condition of success.
- *An intolerance of ambiguity*, or an unwillingness to tolerate ideas that are not concrete and practical. There is also the tendency to conform and not step out of line.
- *A preference for judging ideas rather than generating them.*
- *A belief that we are not creative.* (This issue is covered in greater detail in Chapter 13.)
- *Use of poor creative problem-solving methods* and not having time to think creatively.
- *Stress*: the overstressed person finds it difficult to think objectively at all. Unwanted stress can reduce the quality of all mental processes.
- *Laziness*, or a lack of effort, characterized by a tendency to take the easy option.
- *Habit*, the 'we have always done it this way' syndrome, can be a major block to creativity.
- *A functional fixation*, in terms of how certain elements in the problem are perceived. It is necessary to identify and examine any assumptions that you are making so as to ensure they are not excluding new ideas. Many unconscious assumptions can

restrict thinking – for instance, the use of computers would have been severely restricted if they had been perceived merely as complex adding machines rather than devices to store, manage and manipulate data and images in a sophisticated and flexible way.

- *The 'early bird' syndrome,* or what can be called 'solution fixation', in which the first way of doing something is set in stone without considering alternatives. This premature closing of thoughts can block the way to further searches for other ideas.

Poor Red Light thinking skills

Individuals may underperform or fail to be creative by having poor skills in Red Light thinking. Potential obstacles include the following:

- *Confirmation bias,* where people have a natural propensity to seek confirming evidence and to avoid information with which they feel uncomfortable.
- *Lack of motivation* and any desire to solve the problem. As a result, there is insufficient time or resource dedicated to the follow-through, to see the creative idea to fruition.
- *Following the rules excessively.* Some rules are necessary but they can encourage a form of mental laziness. Creative thought can be hampered by a tendency to conform to the status quo and blindly accept patterns of belief or thought. Values of tradition can also be given too great a priority in the analysis, leading to resistance to change.
- *A focus on the downside rather than the quality of an idea.* Consequently, there is a danger of prejudging ideas and possibly killing off the germ of a good idea.
- *An overreliance on logic,* coupled with an intolerance of subjectivity in the evaluation process. Here there is an overemphasis on the step-by-step approach of logical, analytical thinking at the cost of the Green Light thinking skills of imagination, intuition, and even humour. At its extreme, this restriction could lead to 'paralysis by analysis'.
- *Lack of consultation,* or poor involvement of other team members, which can hamper any subsequent approval or adoption of an idea. Organizational factors, such as autocratic management, can strangle a potential idea at birth. (See Chapter 14.)

- *Excessive reliance on external resources*, such as experts, rather than the skills already within the organization. There may also be a lack of cooperation and trust within an organization.
- *Overemphasis on either competition or cooperation*, leading to ideas either being squeezed out, or selection of the least controversial option.
- *Emphasis on doing rather than thinking*, so that an idea may not be fully thought through. Too many distractions may be put in the way of a cool, clear evaluation of ideas.
- *Being critical and negative.* If there is a desire to minimize your involvement in, and personal contribution to, the task at hand, being critical and negative are the easiest forms of contribution. Criticism is one of the very few ways that non-creative people can achieve something and become influential. There can also be emotional satisfaction to be gained from attacking an idea, which can lead to the perpetrator feeling superior.
- *The insecurities of the expert*, where it is easier to define a position of why something will not work than the potential for its viability. Henry Ford once dismissed 'the expert' as 'someone who will give you six reasons why something will not work'.

POOR MANAGEMENT OF THE CREATIVE PROCESS

Failing to understand the creative process, and its five stages of Information, Incubation, Illumination, Integration and Illustration, can be a major obstacle to creating new ideas. Conversely, understanding this process makes it eminently possible to identify whether or not any of the five stages is responsible for blocking the successful development of an idea – and if so, which one. Table 10.1 lists some practical examples of potential obstacles in each stage.

CULTURAL/SOCIALIZATION PROBLEMS

I was the only child in the East End of London with a triple-barrelled name. At least twice a day, every day, the teachers would remind me of my triple-barrelled name by saying: 'Green-Stop-Daydreaming'.

A personal experience

Table 10.1 *Potential obstacles in the creative process*

Stage in creative process	Potential obstacles
Information	Insufficient information to provide raw material of elements to combine and recombine.
	Failure to define the problem in an ill-structured situation.
Incubation	Not enough time allowed for incubation.
Illumination	Poor Green Light thinking skills.
	Failure to recognize and record illuminations.
Integration	Poor Red Light thinking skills in sifting ideas, analysing their qualities and identifying the added value.
	Poor technical and professional skills, which can hamper translation of ideas into reality.
	The context may be inappropriate for the idea – an idea may be ahead of its time, or overtaken by events.
	Poor organizational skills, resulting in the quality of the ideas not being matched by the calibre of the practical application.
Illustration	Poor technical, professional and presentation skills, which can undermine the inherent qualities of the idea. As a result, the concept may fail to gain necessary approval from decision makers.

Studies on teenagers reveal how our Green Light thinking skills can be dulled. The practical needs of education can contribute to eliminating our talent for fantasy, with its inherent abilities for wonder and curiosity; it is usually easier to ask students to react

with Red Light thinking skills, such as critical comment. Coupled with this is a value and rewards system with an emphasis on control and conformity. And this is imposed at a time in young people's lives when they are at their most self-conscious, and when they are most vulnerable to peer-group pressure to conform.

To improve our creative abilities, the task is not so much putting in new creative skills as unearthing these very talents within us, which may be buried as the result of our upbringing and education, peer-group pressure, or the desire to conform. 'Every child is an artist. The problem is how to remain an artist after growing up', said Picasso.

 When was the last time you wrote a piece of fiction, or painted a picture, or performed music of some sort? What is stopping you doing any of these things today?

OVERCOMING THE OBSTACLES

Having an idea rejected is a common fate for creative practitioners. On reflection, you will usually find it is for the good that the idea was turned down. With the passage of time and further incubation, you can assess the idea's true worth and added value. Nonetheless, there will be occasions when you need to fight with determination to get your creative proposal approved.

In Table 10.2 there is a list of the most common rejections that practitioners are likely to face, together with some initial thoughts on potential responses. It is important always to frame your response with a preface, so as to establish common ground between you and the person with the power to sanction your ideas. Typical bridge-building prefaces could include: 'You are right to be concerned...' or 'It is right to recognize this element...'. Never link your preface with your counter objection by saying 'but' or 'yet', because this immediately signals that you are about to present a contradiction to the other person's point of view.

Table 10.2 *Tactics for overcoming objections*

Objection	Tactics for dealing with objection
1. It won't work.	Get to the bottom of the objection. Use the 'Five Whys' technique; Why won't it work? Why is that? Why…? (etc)
2. We have tried this before and it didn't work.	Identify points common to the situation, and then highlight the differences.
3. We've always done it this way.	Use the 'Five Whys' technique to get to the bottom of the objection. Emphasize the need for changes when appropriate. Minimize (but don't falsify) the risk or scale of the change.
4. It's very creative but it's not for us.	Use the 'Five Whys' technique to get to the bottom of the objection. Identify the brand values of the organization and review whether they have been compromised by the creativity proposal.
5. We're already looking at this.	Check if something similar is indeed already under way, together with any similarities/differences, in order to substantiate the validity of the objection. Check the timescales applicable to the other idea.
6. It will get in the way of existing activities.	Identify the resource requirements and any opportunity costs.
7. The potential targets will not be interested.	Run your idea across contacts in the target audience for their opinion on its merits.
8. It will cost too much.	Identify the resource requirements and provide further details of the logistics involved in developing the idea.

Table 10.2 *Tactics for overcoming objections (continued)*

Objection	Tactics for dealing with objection
9. It's too difficult to do, or this part of it won't work.	Use the 'Five Whys' technique to get to the bottom of the objection.
	Analyse the critical-path requirements of the logistics needed to make the creative proposal work.
	Put the problem into context to lessen potential client anxieties. Look at alternatives for satisfying the objection.
10. This idea has been done before.	Analyse when it was used, and if your potential re-use is compromised in any way. Highlight the new context that you are facing and the fact that there is nothing wrong in borrowing other people's ideas in any way.
11. Another agency's/person's/company's proposals are more creative.	If possible, try to make a genuine comparison. Identify whether or not it is the creative dimension that is being recognized as the distinguishing element, or whether it is some other factor.
	Identify what added value is contained in these other proposals or activities.
12. The idea did not come from me.	Try to overcome the insecurities of the decision makers. Look at inflating their contribution to the idea, or instil a sense of common ownership in the idea.
13. There is no way we can do this.	Consider whether or not any of the above responses are valid to use. If not, accept that sometimes not all of your creative proposals will be accepted, and learn to bounce back.

 Look back on a recent rejection of a creative proposal. Could you have used any of the counter-objections listed in the table above?

Remember, the biggest obstacle to creativity is YOU – which brings us neatly to the next chapter.

SUMMARY

1. Creativity is an inherently uncomfortable task for the brain.
2. Poor skills in any aspect of creativity are major obstacles to coming up with creative solutions.
3. If you know any teachers, ask them to be tolerant of children day-dreaming.

KEY WORDS FOR YOUR CREATIVITY VOCABULARY

- Assumptions.
- Early-bird syndrome.
- 'Five Whys'.
- Ill-structured.
- Well structured.

11

You are never more than 12 feet from an opportunity

You make your own luck in public relations.

(Apologies to Gary Lineker)

In life there are two types of vision providing you with a view of 20:20 clarity. The first is hindsight; you can look back on your life and identify what you should have done, if only you had known then what you know now. With the benefit of hindsight you can see in crystal clear vision the half-chances, opportunities and potential good fortune which were around you, but which you failed to identify at the time.

The other type of vision you possess, to enable you to judge the world and its many opportunities, is sagacity. Sagacity literally means your ability to see the essential truth of a situation. This can act like your opportunity radar, enabling you to spot great creative angles, insights or connections that others have failed to see.

We all have this opportunity radar capable of creating great

results. An old Indian fable about some blind men confronted with an elephant provides a valuable story about how we fail to harness information. Each of the blind men only felt part of the elephant and gave incomplete descriptions, for example one said it was like a spear having felt only its tusk, another said it was like a snake having felt only its tail.

Although each of the blind men gave an accurate description of his immediate perception of an elephant, each failed to realize the true description of what was in front of him.

In one week I came across two statistics. The first was that you are never more than 12 feet away from an electric motor when you are in a building. The other, less savoury statement said that you are never more than 12 feet away from a rat! Believing in synchronicity it can equally be suggested that you are never more than 12 feet away from an opportunity.

THE MILLENNIUM BRIDGE

The Millennium footbridge across the River Thames was closed within three days after its opening in June 2000 because it had a 'wobble'. Engineers subsequently decided that the problem was apparently due to people 'walking the wrong way'. The wobble, or to give the phenomenon its proper title, 'synchronous lateral excitation', was caused by pedestrians unconsciously adjusting their pace to walk in step with the minute vibrations given off by the footbridge when it was being used by a large number of people. This generated slight sideways movements of the bridge making it more comfortable for people to walk in synchronization with the bridge movement. Once the swaying started however, and people tried to counteract it, en masse, they made the problem worse.

In fairness to the engineers, since few footbridges in the world had previously accommodated such large numbers as the Millennium Bridge, the phenomenon was relatively unknown and could not have been easily predicted. The problem of the wobble was, however, self-limiting. Beyond a certain point, it simply becomes impossible to get any more people on the bridge. As it gets fuller, people stop moving and the effect subsides, long before structural safety limits are reached.

The decision was taken to 'repair' the bridge and eliminate the

151

wobble. Some £5 million of repairs later the bridge was reopened in February 2002.

In paradigm terms the 'wobble' was not part of the engineering specification. No one had asked for it and its presence was soon labelled as unwanted, perhaps influenced in some degree by post-Millennium-Dome sensitivities to unsuccessful building projects. But was the wobble a problem?

In paradigm terms a footbridge at the very least has to get people from one side of the river to another without their feet getting wet. In a bigger paradigm it also has to achieve this objective with a relative degree of safety and comfort, hence a rope bridge, although cheaper, would not have been suitable.

Imagine you are the Mayor of an ordinary mediaeval Italian town. Through one office door enters your chief engineer who exclaims: 'Boss, we gotta problem with our bell tower. It's developed a lean! We need to spend five million lire to put it right.' Your head of tourism however shakes his head and says: 'Let's leave it that way – there could be something in it.' Who should the Mayor listen to?

In one paradigm the Millennium Bridge is not just a means of helping people to get across the river. It is also a tourist attraction.

In my view the wobble, instead of being regarded as a problem should have been seen (like the leaning tower of Pisa) as an opportunity. Tourists would have gone out of their way to visit 'the wobbly bridge'. Instead, costly alterations were made, and the scheme came in over budget and delayed, undermining the reputation of British engineering of an otherwise elegant and stylish structure.

Your reality exists in many different levels of paradigm. Some paradigms can be readily identified. Others may require you to be open-minded and tolerant of unusual sources of information. Fundamentally, you need to believe that opportunities are all around you.

The significance of this episode lies in how it highlights that opportunities are there. But they will invariably fail to declare themselves as such. The opportunities that do exist around us – within 12 feet – are concealed, camouflaged, inverted and not explicit.

In my role as a non-executive director on a number of regeneration initiatives I often get frustrated when I come across individuals who say: 'I never had a chance. I never had the opportunity.'

They lead a life as if opportunities come your way at a bus stop marked 'opportunity', where you board a double-decker bus with 'opportunity' on its destination board, and a conductor presents you with 'opportunity' on a plate.

Yet, you might ask yourself, how are we never more than 12 feet from an opportunity? Look around you. If there is anyone else nearby they represent an opportunity with their knowledge, world view, resources they immediately have available to them, along with their contacts and networks. Most people know at least 150 other people. So when you meet someone you are not just meeting them, but potentially their network of contacts as well.

Any object within 12 feet of you represents a solution to a problem. Mundane objects like a table and chair represent design triumphs over the challenges they faced to provide you with added value in some way.

Being creative is not just about generating ideas from scratch. Successful creative individuals are more often marked by their ability to take the creative product of others further forward, by picking up an opportunity and gaining added value.

Every one has sagacity, this ability to sense a bigger picture and it manifests itself in what can be called Small Box and Big Box sagacity.

Small Box sagacity

Each of us will have specific expertise in different areas of life. Your expertise may be in your work in your professional capacity, or in a range of interests such as your favourite film star, football team or hobby. Consider the story told by the great Howard Gossage about his tailor friend who met the Pope. When asked what the Pope was like, the tailor replied: 'He was a 42 medium!'

Most public relations professionals have great expertise in recognizing the media potential of raw information. Our organizations or clients have certain facts about them and as public relations professionals you can read this material and translate it into its potential media interest. When reading a newspaper the public relations practitioner will read it differently from a non-practitioner, with the ability to dissect different sources of material and treatments of stories and issues.

As with exercising a muscle, you can extend your sagacity performance by focusing and exercising. A valuable tip is every

day to look for three good things and three not so good things relevant to your area of expertise. But don't just say 'That's good' and 'That's bad'. Instead, dissect why it is good or why it is bad. One area of my work is brand design. So each day I look out for three good examples of design and build up a reservoir of potential good ideas and also pitfalls and bad practice to avoid. By adopting this habit you sensitize your 'opportunity radar' to pick up potential opportunities that are within 12 feet of you.

From my experience people who are brilliant at spotting opportunities practise seven key habits. Stephen Covey wrote a worldwide best seller *The Seven Habits of Highly Effective People* (Covey, 1989). This represents an opportunity, so the next part of this chapter outlines the seven habits of highly opportunistic people. The 'rules' described below can also help make you more 'lucky'!

1. BE PRINCIPLED

It is curious that if someone is described as 'opportunistic' it is often meant in derogatory terms. The inference being that the person lacks principles. Yet any review of great ideas people – whether they are a scientist, explorer or communicator – all display a great ability to take advantage of opportunities: of being 'opportunistic'.

Yet creative greats, despite being opportunistic, also tend to be highly principled. Their principled nature is based around having a strong sense of mission, belief in their abilities and their quest, and possessing a very strong personal brand based on a clear set of values.

By having a clearly defined personality, or at least a stand on a subject, you act like a beacon or a magnet for other people to come to you. From my own experience I often get approaches along the lines of 'I know you're interested in creativity, and I thought you might like to know about...'

As a creative practitioner, if you have a mission for looking out for new ideas and opportunities you are sending a strong message to yourself, in your intrapersonal communication, to be receptive to stimuli around you. Externally, you are sending out signals for other people to be aware of your personal mission.

Don Sull, an associate professor of management at London Business School, carried out a study, described in an article in the

Financial Times (London), 6 February 2006, on what made 'lucky' managers and businesses. Don Sull highlighted the need for executives to keep their priorities clear. By attempting to pursue too many priorities simultaneously, executives dissipate resources and hinder coordination across units. Managers must exercise ruthless discipline in choosing a small number of objectives to pursue first.

Don Sull added:

> The more successful companies are luckier in the sense that time and again they responded more effectively to unexpected shifts in regulation, technology, competition, macroeconomics or other volatile factors. Such luck is too important to leave to chance. The most successful companies exemplified 'active waiting', an approach to strategy in highly unpredictable markets that consists of anticipating and preparing for threats that executives can neither fully predict nor control.

 What are the important things for you that you want to achieve through your work?

2. BELIEVE THERE ARE OPPORTUNITIES – PRIME YOURSELF

The great opportunity spotters have a major fundamental belief; they believe there are opportunities around. Priming your mind and telling yourself there must be something out there is a form of rocket fuel to keep you going until you eventually find such an opportunity.

You need to have what is called a 'Hibris' attitude to sustain your opportunity hunting. This mental state is like hubris in that it employs a positive arrogance on its ability to achieve success. Yet in a Hibris state the arrogance is focused on the ability to be successful but tempered with humility; you don't know everything, you have a flexibility of thought and respect that there is always something to learn from, even from the unlikeliest of sources.

The Hibris state recognizes that your mental models are best guesses and so you should be on the look out for different ones. When confronted with problems look at the assumptions behind the situation. Look for relationships, and how events fit together,

and consider what are the causes and effects in the situation you are examining. Because of its diversity and breadth of interests a Hibris state is more comfortable with ambiguity and maintains a curiosity with the outside world. It pays particular attention to experiences that contradict your mental models, and seeks to obtain constructive feedback to learn from any experience.

Simon Hughes, of the Central Office of Information, recognizes the importance of keeping an open mind and being receptive to the unlikeliest sources of information. One tool that he uses could be called a 'muse log'. This takes the form of a little black book that he carries around with him and uses to capture thoughts and musings, details and observations. While being all too aware of the huge range of electronic devices that could be used to replace pen and paper, he feels that the act of both physically jotting down these muses and then being able to access them simply by skimming through the pages creates a very different dynamic. It is somehow a more liberating way of lighting upon ideas when compared to being forced to file information away in some form of organized electronic retrieval system.

So what kind of things would you find in his muse log? Observations about who and why someone is the best black hairdresser in Catford, South London, gleaned from an animated discussion overheard on an early morning commute mingle with notes on possible music tracks for events and ideas on change management and leadership. It is a heady mix of musing.

There is no rational hard evidence of such musings being able to lead instantly to an added value opportunity. It does however, harness one of your powerful resources, your intuition; at a subconscious level your mind is registering such information as standing out from the ordinary. This sends out a signal which most people ignore but perceptive people like Simon recognize its longer-term value and significance.

To be a receptive opportunity spotter you need to develop a sense of what Richard Wiseman calls 'mindfulness' – the ability to pay attention to the present rather than thinking and behaving on autopilot. One tip to get yourself out of autopilot mode is to study a familiar object and explore and identify new things you had not noticed before. On one creativity course where participants had to hide their watch from view and describe it in as much detail as possible, one delegate described a watch in incredible detail, only to discover she was wearing a different watch that day!

 Do you have a Hibris attitude to any campaign you are working on?

3. TRY MORE, LITTLE AND OFTEN

If you want to win a raffle or a lottery the more tickets you have, the more chance you have got of winning and the same applies to exercising your creativity and idea sparking; the more ideas you generate and try, the more likely you will get a winner. Certainly, this entails that many of your ideas will not win. Creativity, like the art of selling, is a percentage game; if you try once, don't succeed and give up you will be less successful than your counterparts who keep trying until they get a result. If a campaign idea fails, try again.

4. SEE A BIGGER PICTURE

The blind men in the Indian fable were guilty of looking at a 'little picture', a small box of the situation, seeing only part of a problem. By creating a bigger picture, taking in scenery others might miss in their more blinkered world view, you can spot the opportunities.

Richard Wiseman describes an experiment where a group of people were surveyed and classified into two groups: those who defined themselves as lucky and those who felt they were unlucky. He gave the whole group the same exercise of counting the number of pictures in a newspaper. Unbeknown to the group, there was a large advert in the centre of the newspaper boldly telling them to stop counting and telling them how many pictures there were in the newspaper. Only half the group spotted the advert – it correlated with those who defined themselves as 'lucky'. Wiseman's conclusion is that lucky people have a bigger field of vision in their engagement with the world, perhaps seeing things at the periphery which other more tunnel-vision types would miss.

Don Sull observed how enterprising managers would 'Conduct reconnaissance into the future: send out probes in a few directions to broaden the search for opportunities rather than staking everything on a single way forward.' Often the lead you get for an opportunity is not clearly defined or articulated. Creative

opportunity spotters must also remain alert to anomalies – new information that surprises them or conflicts with expectations. In a fast-moving world of turbulent markets, mental maps quickly become outdated, and anomalies provide clues as to where the map is wrong.

Pressure makes people produce fewer and less diverse ideas. Richard Wiseman, in his book *Did you Spot the Gorilla?* (Wiseman, 2004), describes an experiment where two groups are given the same task of drawing as many different pictures as possible in a number of empty boxes. The first group are told they only have one minute to do the exercise, the second are initially told they have three minutes, but are actually stopped after one minute,

Despite having the same amount of time, the groups produce dramatically different results, with the second group generating more, and more varied, designs. Here, the perception of having an abundance of time is more helpful than the perception of having too little time.

5. USE EVERY CONNECTION

Many of us will have had the experience of working with very negative colleagues who when faced with a problem would give up. My advice to them was to ask someone else for the answer. Nine times out of ten, the person they asked would either know the answer or know someone else who might know. And guess what? These other people will also know around 150 people, so they could possibly plug into these people as well.

 Who do you know who could help you be more successful?

6. FLIP THE NEGATIVE

The author organized a reception event where the British Prime Minister was guest of honour. After the clients had their photo taken he spotted an opportunity to have a photo taken with Mr Blair. Hand outstretched, he asked: 'Mr Blair can I have my photo taken with you please?' Instead of the instant photo flash, he heard

the photographer say: 'Can you hold it there? I have to change my film.' There he was with the most powerful man in Britain. Instead of seizing the moment and saying something profound he lamely blubbered: 'Nice speech'. Afterwards he was annoyed with himself for messing up the opportunity.

The author shared the story in a chance encounter on a train with a friend who ran a publishing company and the idea emerged for a book called *A Minute with Tony Blair*. A range of celebrities and people from all sectors of the community were approached with their responses to the question: 'If you had a minute with Tony Blair what would you say?' The responses ranged from the profound to the comical ('Do you wear boxer shorts?' was one question!).

The resulting book enjoyed great coverage and interest. It also demonstrated how you can turn the negative into the positive.

Opportunistic people have the ability to see 'problems' as opportunities. What 'problems' can you transform into new opportunities?

7. BE PERSISTENT

Opportunistic people don't give up. If faced with a straight 'No', or other rejection there are always ways to try again, or make a different approach. Simply to keep turning up often leads to success.

8. DO MORE

It was mentioned earlier that there are seven habits of opportunistic people. Creative practitioners are also marked out by doing more, going beyond what was asked or expected. The eighth factor is that outstanding creative results invariably come from someone driven to do more. Look back on any outstanding success you have been involved with and you probably went the extra mile in some way.

Furthermore, when you have a gut feeling about something, learn to spot the feeling and trust your instincts. If you come across an opportunity that on the surface has little obvious added value,

but you feel 'there could be something in it', that is a sign from your intuition. Learn to be aware of these signals. And listen to them.

OVERVIEW

By developing your sagacity skills to spot opportunities you will be able to harness the many potential ideas around you waiting to be harnessed and developed to achieve great creative results. There is a tendency to regard the creative act as always working with a blank canvas. In reality, great added value results are more often achieved by surfing with someone else's idea or opportunity.

SUMMARY

1. The creative person is often an outstanding opportunity hunter, spotter and harvester of other people's ideas.
2. Being opportunistic does not make you unprincipled.
3. Outstanding creative practitioners often have a strong sense of mission or purpose in their life which acts like a magnet to attract potential opportunities.
4. Belief in the availability of opportunities, the ability to turn negatives into positives, trying more, little and often, seeing a bigger picture, using every connection, flipping the negative, persistence and going the extra mile are the characteristics of the successful creative opportunity spotter.

KEY WORDS FOR YOUR CREATIVITY VOCABULARY

- Sagacity.
- Surfing.

12

The 'creative diamond'

> Flexible thinking is the most powerful tool you have to create and manage your future. In fact, it's the only tool.
>
> *Comment to creativity course delegates*

The 'creative diamond' is represented by your four quotients – this is the model underpinning what makes any person or team creative.

Intelligence quotient is well known as one measure of ability. You also have quotients in your emotional, vision and adversity skills which, when working together with your intelligence, enable you to create ideas.

The way you think is shaped by the way you use these different quotients. Each challenge you face is different. Sometimes you will need to generate new insights, new options. Other times you may need to explore the full logical facts, or need emotionally to get under the skin of a situation, or be determined to overcome opposition to get your way or deliver your solution.

The outstanding public relations creative is marked by being flexible and being able to secure the optimum balance between

these different resources to meet the needs of a specific time or situation. Different people will be suited to different situations, because of their varying strengths in their resource quotients. A dynamic, powerful deliverer of an idea may be ideal for executing an idea but in another context someone who is low key, trusting and can empathize may be more appropriate in getting the involvement of others to come up with ideas.

THE FOUR Qs

The four quotients can be visualized as the four points of a diamond.

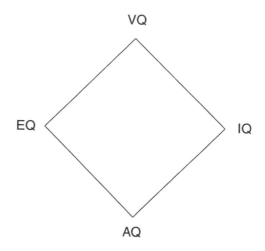

Figure 12.1

How do these different quotients work when it comes to being creative?

Intelligence quotient – IQ

Outstandingly creative people can use their IQ skills for information gathering to identify new trends and developments as well as for understanding the rational basis of the assignment and objectives they face in their communications.

The need for analysis can also be critical for planning for contingencies, preparing for any situations that may occur and cause difficulties. Your IQ skills will help you define the challenge, by helping to establish specific objectives you need to achieve, and also grasp the key facts of a situation by breaking information into component parts and identifying individual relationships between the different elements.

 Do you have sufficient facts and details about the campaign you are working on? What more can you find out?

Emotional quotient – EQ

Emotions rather than facts are more likely to provide the reality of a situation.

Daniel Goleman, in his book *Emotional Intelligence* (Goleman, 1996), first defined emotional quotient (EQ) as the ability to sense, understand and apply the power and acumen of emotions as a source of human energy, information, trust, creativity and influences.

Using your EQ skills you can establish the bigger picture of any situation going beyond the obvious logical elements. Your EQ enables you to deal with ambiguity, to make positive use of potential opportunities inherent in any situation.

Harnessing your EQ skills will enable you to encourage openness and information sharing and adapt to the needs of different audiences.

 Have you sufficiently taken into account the emotional dimension in any campaign you have been involved with?

Vision quotient – VQ

Vision is crucial to success, whether the task is running a country or organization, or issuing a press release; they all need a vision to be fulfilled. If, for example you are producing a press release and you have a limited vision of its potential success, you are likely to have a self-fulfilling prophecy. The more coherent and defined your goal the more likely you are to achieve it. As Oscar

163

Hammerstein observed: If you don't have a dream, how are you going make your dream come true?

Creative public relations communicators possess a vision of a potential positive outcome to their communications challenge. Their VQ contains two elements; the sense of a horizon: of where they want to be with their creative product, underpinned by specific goals that are stepping stones to reaching the vision.

Positive thinking fuels vision. Yet pessimism or scepticism can be good. Either can provide a reality check. To deliver a creative product successfully you need to know about realistic threats and challenges.

Pessimism is unhelpful when it is made permanent – creating a mindset of 'thinking it will never happen', or pervasive – where whatever we do we think it will never work. The solution is to harness 'pit-stop pessimism' – as a quick reality check – and then move on.

Outstanding creative practitioners think beyond immediate issues by using their vision to focus on future benefits, maintaining a positive outlook to overcome any negative short-term issues.

 Do you have a strong vision for your next creative product?

Adversity quotient – AQ

Being creative, creating and delivering new ideas will inevitably mean you run into obstacles. A crucial talent of the creative practitioner is not to give in – your AQ. This is the will to succeed, resilience, the ability to bounce back and not be deterred in your quest.

Anything you have done well in your life you will have achieved because it had some underlying meaning to you. The challenge for the successful communicator is to ascribe positive meaning to any task. During a creativity training course for a group of radio advertising creatives one delegate recalled how he struggled to come up with ideas for a campaign to recruit Special Constables (unpaid volunteer police officers). The guy remembered the thought process going through his head: Why would anyone want to be an unpaid copper? He had successfully created, for himself, negative meaning to the assignment – which formed a barrier for his normal creative flow.

He could have reframed the brief by identifying a value which had personal meaning to him, such as: 'I want to live in a community where people can feel safe'. He then could have embarked on the job of generating ideas to address the task.

Outstanding creatives combine the ability to stick with things and also know when to drop something and walk away. The more options and opportunities you have, the more flexibility you have at your disposal.

Your AQ skills enable you to respond positively to changes or setbacks, personally and corporately. If you are weak you will let yourself down, undermine any confidence the media may have in you, and also damage the reputation of your organization. You need an inner toughness to see you through these situations. It is only when the crisis is over that you have the time to reflect and critically analyse your own performance. When the dust has settled, it can be useful to talk to the key contacts to get some feedback, good and bad.

 Have you asked yourself: Why is this next task important to me? Can you inflate its sense of meaning to you?

THE FOUR Qs OVERVIEW IN CREATIVITY – GETTING THE BALANCE RIGHT

Which resources are most helpful? Table 12.1 sets out key resources to use in different situations.

THE RIGID, INFLEXIBLE MIND

Having rigid, limiting mental models will hold back your communications – and your life. It can severely hamper your ability to achieve any form of empathy – the ability to put yourself in another person's position – with your target. You can recognize that you are displaying the typical characteristics of an inflexible mind if you:

● insist your ideas are the only reality;
● have a narrow set of interests to ensure that you ignore a lot of experiences;

Table 12.1 *Key resources to use in different situations*

Situation	Key resources to use
Research/factual story	Your IQ skills to analyse the significance and understand the subject matter and its context are the fundamental starting point for your communications in this situation. By relying too much on IQ, and failing to translate your expert knowledge to other less knowledgeable people, you can hinder your communications.
Human interest stories	Your EQ skills – your ability to empathize, get under the skin of your subject and understand what other people would be interested in on an emotional level are crucial for these opportunities.
Crisis situation	Your AQ skills – your ability to cope with pressure, stand up and fight your corner if necessary and bounce back from adversity are all critical in a crisis. Your VQ skills can also be helpful to look beyond the immediate problems and any short-term difficulties and to depicit a future horizon to move towards.
New campaign	Your VQ skills in being able to paint a new world with the success of your campaign already envisaged in your mind will help propel you and your colleagues forward in delivering communications.

- do not tolerate ambiguity and jump in haste to conclusions;
- devise creative excuses to explain things away when they do not go as you planned;
- use lots of negative determining words in your language, such as 'never' and many universals, like 'always';
- are quick to generalize;
- set up plenty of one-sided, unfocused experiences to provide evidence of your ideas or blame failures squarely on others and do not examine other possible factors;
- think solely in straight lines of cause and effect;

- are never curious and never update your beliefs in the light of experience.

Whenever as a communicator you are faced with limiting mental models, whether it is something within yourself or from someone else, here are four ways to challenge your mental map:

- Who says?
- So what?
- Why not?
- What evidence have you got?

By recognizing that your creative thinking is made up of an interplay between the four different quotients, you can gain an intrapersonal insight into your own thinking. Is your thinking dominated by one quotient? Do you make insufficient use of certain quotients: does your thinking lack vision, intelligence, emotion or robustness with adversity?

By having a greater understanding of how you think, you can manage this dimension. You will also appreciate what characterizes your own brand of thinking.

SUMMARY

1. The outstanding creative is flexible and able to secure the optimum balance between different resources to meet the needs of a specific time or situation.
2. The creative practitioner can draw upon skills in IQ, EQ, VQ and AQ.

KEY WORDS FOR YOUR CREATIVITY VOCABULARY

- Intelligence quotient.
- Emotional quotient.
- Vision quotient.
- Adversity quotient.

13

The creative individual

Einstein's brain weighed 1,400 grams – the same size as the average human brain. Certainly, he was a great creative genius, but it was not as a result of a superhumanly sized brain. Just think: you probably have the same sized brain as Einstein – a tremendous asset at your disposal. Yet what can you do to improve your individual creative talents as a public relations practitioner?

Here are 10 characteristics of creative public relations people. By considering how you currently measure up to each, you can identify any weaknesses in your make-up. This can then be used to improve your performance, and mark the start of a new, more creative, you.

1. BE UNCOMFORTABLE

I don't like trying anything new that I cannot do.

PR trainee, aged 41

Public relations people often say: 'I am not creative', or 'I do not have a creative bone in my body', or 'I just do not seem able to come up with ideas'.

After the first series of my creativity training courses, I was faced with the problem of some people who, despite being taught about the nature of creativity and the creative process, and despite being armed with a series of tips and techniques, continued to act like 'wallflowers'; they were still unable to demonstrate any significant level of creative ability. Well, a message to all these people is that YOU DECIDE whether or not you want to be creative. The root cause of you not being creative is your inherent belief. You can choose to believe you are creative.

What you are able to do in life comes from your skill, backed by your core beliefs and values. These values and beliefs are generalizations that we make about ourselves, others, and the world around us, and they are the principles by which we act. It is possible to change beliefs – for example, it is unlikely you believe in Father Christmas, though once you did. While we do have core beliefs that are fixed and important to us, we can also be flexible about what we choose to believe in certain areas of our lives. These beliefs can act as self-fulfilling prophecies.

Each of us has what is called a 'Comfort Zone' in how we think and – more importantly – how we address any new challenges. Think back to the time when you sat behind the steering wheel of a car for your very first driving lesson. You were probably terrified at the thought of the car moving off, and very much aware that you were not in control. Yet, after several years of driving, you can no doubt do it with very little concern or trepidation. You have moved inside your Comfort Zone.

Similarly, looking back to my first week working in public relations, I recall the sheer hell I went through drafting my very first press release: having previously written numerous articles for student newspapers, this would be the very first time my work would be scrutinized by 'a proper public relations professional'. But I have progressed since then: I can deal with a very intense PR crisis situation, or come up with creative proposals for a major campaign, and such events are well within my Comfort Zone. My most recent stressful experience – and there are still some, of course – was having to e-mail a PowerPoint presentation, because it was a task I did not at the time have the technical knowledge or experience to carry out.

Fear of failure and of not being in control of a situation are the biggest factors in limiting the size of our Comfort Zones. How many times in our working day do we say to ourselves: 'I'm not going to be able to do this', or 'I just cannot seem to come up with the right idea'. How can we address this problem, which is in some way holding us back? A valuable tip is to deliberately step outside your Comfort Zone by doing a task you do not feel comfortable about. Accept that you may not do it right first time, learn from the experience, do it again but apply the lessons learnt until eventually you feel more comfortable doing it. That is, after all, how most of us acquire new skills – whether it is learning to drive or being creative.

The inner circle in Figure 13.1 depicts your Comfort Zone. Within this are activities that you are comfortable doing. The outer circle in the diagram represents tasks and activities that you feel *un*comfortable about. In the circles on Figure 13.1, write in five things you feel comfortable about and five things that are outside your Comfort Zone in your job. Set yourself the goal of expanding your Comfort Zone over the next 12 months by attempting one or more of the tasks currently outside it.

In our creativity training courses with public relations staff from consultancies and in-house departments, the five fears that feature most prominently are:

- public speaking;
- coming up with an idea under pressure;
- having to contradict a senior manager or client;
- cold-calling a potential sales prospect or journalist;
- networking.

Figure 13.1 *Your Comfort Zone*

Change your attitude

Experts reckon that 85 per cent of your success or failure is down to attitude. Remember, even if you do something new badly, you have helped expand your Comfort Zone. This is why there is no such thing as failure, only feedback. The trick is to live with the possibility of making mistakes and to learn how to fail intelligently.

The Irish novelist James Joyce noted: 'A man's errors are his portals of discovery.' Thomas Edison is the most commonly quoted example of someone who learnt from his failures: he is reckoned to have known several thousand ways how *not* to build a light bulb before accomplishing his major invention.

Limit the risk

You may be thinking that it is all very well to write in a book that it is OK to make mistakes, but you think that in the real world you will get crucified by your manager, client, or colleagues. The trick is to use quality control measures for evaluating ideas and concepts (described in Chapter 8 on Red Light thinking) or to minimize the scale of the risk.

In consultancy, you may want to attempt new things, or enable more junior staff to stretch themselves by giving them opportunities on a low-value, or even a nil-fee, client. In-house departments could look at working with a third party, such as a charity of community initiative, to try something different.

Another safeguard is to take out what I call 'creative insurance': if you are doing anything like a creative photocall, always remember to have a second photographic pose done, the 'banker shot', to fall back on if the creative photo pose has not turned out as planned.

Reframing

A further tip when addressing tasks you do not feel comfortable doing is to 'reframe' the way you see it. What you are essentially doing is redefining the paradigm, which, as we have noted before, will determine your subsequent creative solutions. For example, when having to make cold sales calls, consider the job as a percentages game: successful selling can require making a large number of

calls in order to land new business from just a small number of customers. Each call, no matter how unsuccesful, will lead you a step nearer to a successful contact.

Another common complaint from practitioners is making follow-up calls to journalists after issuing a press release. Rather than seeing this as an isolated, irksome task, the practitioner should reframe it as a vital link in the whole process of a successful media relations campaign.

2. BE A PIG, A MULE AND ZEBEDEE

Veni, vidi, velcro (I came, I saw, I stuck with it).
Graffiti I would have written in an ancient Roman toilet

There is much to be gained from the analogy of the role of the hen and the pig in the production of the great English breakfast: in playing their respective parts for the egg and bacon, the hen is involved but the pig is committed.

It is vital for successful creative public relations to have a high degree of commitment to the outcome of the task. At a Chartered Institute of Public Relations conference there was a debate along the lines of 'Should practitioners be genuinely committed to the cause they are promoting?' During the debate, someone put forward the counterargument that you did not need to be committed, using the example of his work for a client who was a chewing-gum manufacturer. The practitioner did not chew gum, but argued that he could still do a professional job for the client concerned, without having a commitment to the client's tastes or to the client's vision of a world full of gum chewers.

Yet both camps missed the point that commitment is essential for successful creative public relations. The commitment, however, is to the success of your creative and professional efforts rather than to the goals of the cause or organization you are working for. In the example of the conference debate, you do not necessarily have to be committed to advancing the interests of the world's gum chewers, but the task of providing a creative and professional job must have some meaning in order for you to generate a level of commitment to the task.

Involvement

The issue of involvement is fundamental, whether or not you share the goals of an organization you are working for. There must be a degree of what can be called 'intrinsic motivation', an interest in a task for its own sake rather than for any 'extrinsic motivation', such as money or sharing the external values of the organization.

You must have something at stake – so that you will be motivated to make your idea successful. The humorist Clive James recalls in his memoirs (the *Falling Towards England* volume, 1991) how he failed to land a job with an advertising agency when he first arrived in Britain from Australia, as a result of this very question of motivation:

> He [the agency boss] had no doubt that I could write Australia's answer to *Paradise Lost* in the evenings while concurrently promoting cornflakes all day... What he was after, however, was someone who wanted to do nothing else except promote cornflakes. They wanted someone for whom the poetry was not separate from the cornflakes, but actually in the cornflakes and of the cornflakes.

Determination

In addition to commitment is the quality of determination. Jeremy Isaacs, the former head of Channel 4 television in Britain, describes working with creative people and is quoted by Winston Fletcher as observing: 'The most important way in which creative people are distinguished is by their single-mindedness, their belief that the beauty of a project, or the excellence of a script or film, has to be realized to the ultimate degree.' James Dyson, the British inventor, puts his success down to stubbornness when he claims in his autobiography *Against The Odds* (1997) that he possesses 'nothing but the virtues of a mule'. You will no doubt be able to recall colleagues who shared this single-mindedness. They were often described as 'pains'. There is nothing worse than working with a prima donna, especially one without the creative talent to justify it. Yet belief in what you are doing, and the mule-like qualities of determination to stick with it through thick and thin, are vital characteristics of the outstanding creative person.

From my experience, creative people do not necessarily score well in made-up exercises in creativity, such as doing tests with

matchsticks to solve a problem, because they see through the artificiality of the task and are, therefore, not really committed to coming up with a solution. They will need to be given goals within the task, such as making it fun, interesting, or even competitive, in order to captivate them.

It is inevitable that practitioners will not succeed with every creative idea they are keen to bring to fruition. As highlighted in the Illustration stage of the five 'I's creative process, even the most successful of creative practitioners feel their best work is in the wastepaper basket. Matched with the determination to succeed is the ability to bounce back, or what can be called the 'Zebedee Factor' (after the spring-loaded character in the children's television series *The Magic Roundabout,* who bounced in at the end of every episode).

All the creative practitioners interviewed for this book constantly have what they regard as their best ideas rejected, yet they bounce back again and again to grasp a new opportunity. As the playwright Tom Stoppard has observed: 'Every exit is an entrance to somewhere else.' History has many examples of ideas coming through that were deemed as failures, thanks to the determination of their originators. In the world of film both *ET* and *Star Wars,* for example, were rejected by the major studios. The ancient Japanese proverb of 'Fall down seven times and stand up eight' is an apt one for the successful creative practitioner.

Inevitably there will be times when you are faced with situations where the egg from the hen is on your face. The only thing to do then is to take solace from the words of Sting in his song, *An Englishman in New York,* in which he sings: 'It takes a man to suffer ignorance and smile.' And bounce back again.

3. HAVE A POSITIVE ANCHOR AND BE ROBERT DAVY

How would Robert Davy start this section?

A question

We all have role models and mentors in our careers – people we may have worked with or know of; or someone famous in a

historical sense, whom we respect for their work or influence. But how many effectively harness these role models to improve their creativity?

A role model can be a real person, or an imaginary one, and can be used as an aspirational tool, to inspire and encourage incremental creative thoughts by helping to answer the question: 'What would so-and-so do in this situation?' Role models can also be used to detach any feelings of individual inadequacies or anxieties about the task in hand.

Having a role model is more than just a device for generating ideas. It can be there, day in and day out, to influence and guide us in our working lives, both from actual experiences and also by conjecturing how they would handle a particular situation. Early in my career I was fortunate to have the late Robert Davy as a boss. Robert had extensive public relations experience around the world in consultancy, in-house work and government, latterly at the Cabinet Office. Every day the question is posed by me: 'What would Robert do here?' At the very worst, all that may emerge is a smile as I recall Robert's unique style of work. At best, it generates a feeling that a good idea may emerge.

Positive anchors

Reference has been made earlier in the book to 'positive anchors' – see Chapter 5 for the 'Disney strategy' showing how you can harness anchoring to maximum effect. The next paragraph is also guaranteed to make you feel good.

Anchoring is a concept widely used in selling to improve salespeople's performances. Shut your eyes and think about your favourite holiday. Try to recall it and make your memory of it as vivid as possible – the sights, sounds, smells – and breathe in as deeply and slowly as possible. Keep that image in your mind for a few seconds longer. Now open your eyes. At the end of this, you have automatically made yourself feel better: the world looks better, and you are in a better position to tackle whatever task you are facing.

Anchoring is a technique to elicit memories by verbal or non-verbal cues, using certain words or gestures that are associated with a pleasurable emotion. For example, getting ready to go out on a Saturday night, you may put on aftershave or perfume. Immediately, the smell brings on the feeling of a social occasion

and good times ahead – so the smells could be used in another context to evoke this feeling.

The use of anchoring is not only great for motivation and for making yourself very persuasive, but also for triggering specific skills within you, such as being creative. I have specific ties for certain tasks. Running a consultancy, I have a 'new business tie' that is worn for pitches – and that has never been beaten in a pitch. Sure, there were times I did not win the pitch, but then I find there is a reason why the magic of the tie did not work. This may seem from the outside as just superstitious nonsense. Yet, internally, it is used as a tool to generate a positive sense of mental well-being for the task in hand. I also have a 'creative tie', which is associated in my mind with great acts of creativity.

4. OVERFLOW YOUR JUG

It's not just in Batley that you need variety.

A reflection

Creative individuals, with their outpourings of new ideas, are rather like a jug overflowing. Yet a jug can only overflow if it is receiving a larger inflow of liquid. You cannot expect to be overflowing with ideas if you are not receiving a larger inflow of new ideas and information.

If you want to be creative, it is no good going to a desert island, shutting yourself away for several months, and expecting to come up with a new idea for your work. While there may be some merit in creating an incubation period with low cortical arousal (see Chapter 5), in order to think creatively you need to stimulate your 10 billion-plus brain cells with a fresh inflow of information. This does not mean chaining yourself to a desk and going through piles of books, because looking for information from unusual sources can trigger creative activity. As the distinguished Yorkshire journalist David Marsh said to me: 'Anyone can look for fashion in a clothes shop or art in a gallery. The creative person looks for art in a street market and fashion in a bus station.'

In Chapter 4, on the creative process, the Information stage was identified as the crucial first step in generating and creating new ideas. It is vital that you expose yourself to as wide a range of experiences and information as possible. Try these stimulants.

Reading

Read as many newspapers as possible. It is invaluable, because they are catalogues of ideas and opportunities. Many of my most successful media relations coups have achieved outstanding coverage from opportunistic responses to stories spotted during my early morning scanning of the newspapers – for example, the idea of a sports footwear client supplying a special pair of golf shoes to a 6 feet 10 inches giant golfer whose large feet hampered his playing prospects; or the Yorkshire girls' grammar school that produced musical instruments from garden implements, which inspired a recycled orchestra of classical musicians playing *Greensleeves* in a very successful series of regional launches for a recycling company.

Furthermore, by reading newspapers regularly, you can have a go at 'surfing'. This is where you identify a particular item of topical interest and link your own message or promotion with this issue of wider interest. (In this context, therefore, it is *not* the same as surfing the internet – but see below.) By surfing you can gain added value for your particular story, capitalizing on the larger news value of the topical item. What has Leonardo di Caprio got to do with insurance? For a bank client who was launching a new business insurance service with low news value, added value and extra media coverage were obtained by linking it with the then topical interest in the launch of the film *Titanic*. The news release tied the insurance story angle to the sinking of the great liner with the intro: 'When the Titanic sank in 1912, fortunately for its owners, the White Star Line, it had adequate insurance cover for its liabilities. However, how many modern-day small businesses could cope if faced with their own equivalent of the iceberg?'

Another obvious area for surfing of a different kind is to use new media. For example, searches on the internet for specific information – or even just a random search – can yield interesting results.

Go beyond news and current affairs. Biographies offer valuable inspiration, and even opportunities to develop role models. The obituary columns in quality broadsheets are a rich source of potted biography, read in minutes, of people whose life's work can offer inspiration, new insight, and the odd new idea to borrow and adapt.

Read selectively from a wide range of sources. You might not expect Walt Disney to have been a typical *Reader's Digest* reader, but he once gave it an outstanding endorsement: 'Your

177

imagination may be creaky, or timid, or dwarfed, or frozen at points. The *Reader's Digest* can serve as a gymnasium for its training.' There are other potential gymnasia for developing new ideas. Every town centre in Britain used to have its *Socialist Worker* newspaper sellers, and I used to buy a copy every so often – not because of a belief in a Far Left takeover of British institutions of power but to spot new trends that might be emerging as mainstream issues. Looking back to the early 1980s, by scanning through the small ads in these newspapers you were able to identify the emergence later in the decade of the Green movement, as well as animal rights campaigning and vegetarianism. With this type of research, you can be creatively at the forefront of new issues and trends.

My wife is irritated, whenever we go anywhere, by my picking up any leaflets on display. If it is a competition leaflet, the small print is examined, including how the competition is structured and organized. Later I will no doubt have a client who will say: 'We are thinking of running a competition…', and will be offered a quick response of: 'Well, you could organize it this way or run it like this…'. I am not spontaneously coming up with creative ideas but have made myself, wherever possible, reasonably authoritative in my field, and can draw upon this knowledge to give the impression of being creative.

One final tip. When you are reading the daily 'creative catalogues of ideas', do it by scanning the pages, reading just the headlines and intros to each story. And do it standing up. This may be less comfortable and more tiring, but will help you focus on the task and complete it without distraction, in the least possible time.

A variety of media

Although practitioners may take in several newspapers a day, how many read a variety of papers, tabloids as well as broadsheets? The *Sun*, for example, should be scanned every day – for professional reasons, and in much the same way as the agents in the film *Men in Black* read the *National Enquirer* for news on alien encounters. Listen to several different radio stations every week. Try to take in media you do not normally choose. For example, if you are a young executive, listen occasionally to the classical music channel Classic FM – it may have an older age profile for its audience but

there may be sponsorship opportunities, or other ideas you would normally miss.

A variety of experiences

Travel broadens the mind, goes the adage. Even armchair travel will broaden your horizons. Keeping your eyes, ears and mind open to the new experiences offered by new surroundings is important for the public relations professional.

Visit art exhibitions, films, theatres, displays. All offer new material, providing new elements to combine with others, to help you create new ideas. When was the last time you visited an art exhibition? You should set yourself a target of going somewhere you would not otherwise have gone, at least every three months, say.

A variety of people

People are a great source of inspiration. Outstanding creative geniuses were not often isolated figures but conspicuously surrounded themselves with the best minds of their time in a wide range of fields.

The one area where in-house practitioners are sometimes in danger of lagging behind their consultancy colleagues is in their more limited networking. This is an essential task for consultants, driven by the need to acquire new business leads and opportunities. It has the added benefit of helping your creativity: the more people from more varied backgrounds that you meet, the bigger your potential to create new ideas.

When you meet successful people, ask them directly about the secrets of their success. You will be surprised how forthcoming even the most outstanding of people will be to this request to talk about themselves. There is much to be gained by associating yourself with those who are creative and positive thinking.

A variety of perspectives

Getting away from your routine can lead you to new thoughts. How about coming into work by a different route? Extend this to where you normally sit in your office or at meetings – try moving elsewhere in the room. It is surprising how new perspectives trigger new insights. Write your ideas down, not using your usual hand. Some writers claim that by using a different hand they

access a different part of the brain. I suspect it is more likely that, as a result of establishing a sense of detachment, they are helping to suspend judgement, and to dissociate themselves from anxieties and inhibitions while dealing with new thoughts and ideas.

5. TAKE YOUR HUNCHES TO LUNCH

I knew I shouldn't have trusted her after she served tinned carrots for dinner.

An observation

The Incubation stage of the creative process highlights how practitioners should make full use of their brainpower by employing their subconscious, ie by planting ideas and letting them germinate and develop. A further dimension to the power of the subconscious is the role of the hunch. A hunch is an intuitive feeling, characterized by an inability to put our finger precisely on a reason, or to explain why we have a feeling towards a particular issue, thing or person.

For the logical mind, the advice to trust your hunches may be outside the Comfort Zone. Yet hunches should not be regarded as a form of emotional judgement. Rather, the brain absorbs certain information and is not able to provide an explanation for how it has been rationalized in the conscious mind. Research has shown that we receive an estimated 2+ million bits of information every minute through our various senses, but we can consciously handle only 300–599 bits in this time. The remaining vast amount of data is filtered and dealt with at an unconscious level. The feeling manifested by the hunch therefore does have some basis in reality.

It is essential to learn and trust your gut instincts – or what an American friend recently described as 'power hunches'. David Ogilvy, the great advertising guru, is emphatic when he observes in *Advertising* (Ogilvy, 1987): 'Steep yourself in your subject, work like hell, and love, honour and obey your hunches.' A hunch is creativity trying to tell you something. You should aim to keep an open mind and be alert for the hunches you have.

Nonetheless, effective harnessing of your hunches does require a sound basis of professional skills and knowledge to enable you to discriminate, endorse, or reject those coming your way.

6. WORK, WORK – AND WORK

I genuinely believe I don't really work that hard.
Confession of a workaholic

Creative public relations people are rather like the man with the violin who stopped a passer-by in London to ask: 'How do you get to the Royal Albert Hall?' and got the reply: 'Practise.' Contrary to a popular stereotype of creative people as somewhat airy-fairy in outlook, an essential characteristic of the outstandingly creative individual is simply that they work hard. Thomas Edison noted: 'Genius is 99 per cent perspiration and 1 per cent inspiration.' The only place you will find success before work is in the dictionary.

Yet many creative practitioners are regarded as almost lucky in the way they come up with idea after idea. Many creative practitioners will be able to relate to Gary Player, the South African golfer, who said: 'The harder I practise, the luckier I get!' Being outstandingly creative is hard work, whether it is standing up reading the 'catalogues of ideas' every day, or working into the early hours to develop your precious idea into a reality. There is no substitute for this.

7. BE A PROFESSOR OF PUBLIC RELATIONS AND *PARLEZ* PR

You would expect a surgeon who was operating on you to read *The Lancet*. When was the last time you read a book or magazine on PR?
Open question to creativity course delegates

Have you ever worked with a graphic artist or designer and been driven crazy by their inability to spell? They are not necessarily stupid, but rather they have the ability to see words in their totality as shapes, as visual elements. They can present words in a certain way as an image, but not as a collection of specific individual letters that have an established sequence of spelling. In effect, graphic designers *parlent* a language of images and pictures.

Creative people have the ability to visualize in their medium. You may relate to that experience when someone explains the facts of a situation and you almost instanteously visualize in your

mind the potential media coverage, a picture of how it would materialize as a news story. What you are effectively doing is *parlez*-ing in an important medium used by public relations practitioners.

To visualize effectively the public relations potential of a situation, and have the ability to come up with outstanding creative solutions, is primarily achieved by becoming, in effect, a 'professor of PR'. By possessing extensive, well-organized, professional knowledge, you will have an edge to your creativity and the ability to come up with creative solutions for the new tasks that you face.

Extensive knowledge in itself does not guarantee creativity of a high calibre. But it is the necessary precondition for high-level performance because your brain is able to call upon more effective solutions to a problem. Research on problem solving has shown that novices tend to use weak strategies, while experts are able to focus on deeper, underlying principles affecting a situation. Whereas the beginner's mind will contain many possibilities, the expert's mind will focus on a few, higher-quality alternatives.

This is not to say that any young public relations practitioner cannot be creative. Many young people produce illuminations of great originality and value. Yet their lack of experience in the Integration and Illustration stages of the creative process could possibly inhibit the full potential of their creative work. Nonetheless, they are likely to improve their ability to produce works of greater merit as they acquire more skill and experience – Mozart was a typical example of a child prodigy as an outstanding and gifted performer, but his first world-class work was produced at the age of 17, when he had gained at least 10 years' experience of his craft.

The question remains: why are some people who possess great technical knowledge and experience in public relations still not creative? The answer to this is in the next section.

8. IS YOUR ESCALATOR A STAIRWAY?

The question is not whether the glass is half-empty or half-full, but is it a glass of water?

An observational question

A department store in Hong Kong was once reputed to have placed a sign on a broken-down escalator, which read: 'This escalator is temporarily a stairway'. For the creative public relations practitioner, an ability to tolerate ambiguities is an important facet. The Roman god Janus had two faces looking in opposite directions. This image has led some experts to define 'Janusian thinking' as the capacity to conceive and utilize simultaneously two or more opposite or contradictory ideas, concepts or images.

Seeing the paradox of a situation is at the crux of creative thinking when you may be entertaining two different – often contradictory – notions at the same time. Creative people have a flexibility enabling them to deal with half an idea, even half-emerged facts, coupled with the ability to abandon old ways of thinking and to initiate different directions. The talent, as the Waterboys' song goes, of being able to see 'the whole of the moon', while others can only see the crescent, is a fundamental feature of the outstanding practitioner.

Creativity was earlier defined as bringing together two disconnected notions or elements. Therefore, the more flexibility you can display in bringing together a wider variety of elements, the greater your ability to generate a bigger number of ideas with a higher potential for originality and added value.

The flexible mind has the ability to identify different elements that:

- appear to be irrelevant and, on the surface, bear no relation to the task in hand;
- do not relate to you personally, either in time or space. This may be something from history, or from the other side of the world, which contains an element that you have identified as having potential;
- originate from a source that may lack any authority or legitimacy. A child may come up with an idea that everyone else dismisses, and you say: 'Hold on, there just might be something in this';
- may fall within a sphere completely outside your professional or technical background. 'What would the public relations person know about this?' was a put-down I once received at a management meeting;
- could only be identified by a hunch you may have about a

situation, where its real potential is not immediately recognizable or easily accessible.

Why is it that some practitioners who possess extensive professional knowledge and experience are still not creative? The answer is in their flexibility of thought – or lack of it. The ability of creative practitioners to adjust their learning state when handling tasks distinguishes them from non-creative practitioners. Table 13.1 defines these different learning states.

Table 13.1 *Four stages of learning skills*

Learning stage	Characteristics
Unconscious incompetence	You do not realize that you do not know. For example, the small child at the steering wheel of its parents' car, pretending to drive, is blissfully unaware it lacks the necessary skills to drive.
Conscious incompetence	You realize your shortcomings, that you do not have the necessary knowledge or skills to attempt or complete a task successfully.
Conscious competence	You know how to do something, but you have to concentrate to do it right.
Unconscious competence	You can do something without thinking about it.

Experienced practitioners who are good at their job display unconscious competence; they can tackle many tasks almost without thinking about them because they possess the necessary skills, confidence and experience. Furthermore, when looking at a new problem or an issue in a new way, creative practitioners have the skill to switch back more quickly than their non-creative peers to a more basic learning state.

The entrepreneur Richard Branson once observed in a radio interview I heard: 'It is better to ask stupid questions than to make stupid mistakes.' The prime feature of creative practitioners is the ability to speedily re-equip themselves with ignorance; to identify

what new information, perspectives or skills are required. As a result, they more readily avoid applying old solutions to new issues and problems.

In addition to the four stages of learning skills given in Table 13.1, there is a further stage – conscious supercompetence. This is defined by the speed with which outstanding practitioners can adjust their learning state. Other less creative practitioners will change their learning state more slowly, and be less able to respond with new ideas or new ways of doing things. The conscious supercompetent practitioners possess high levels of skill and experience, but know they need to couple these with the talent to look at a task in a completely new way and, subsequently, quickly switch back to an earlier learning state. Figure 13.2 shows how conscious supercompetent practitioners can quickly move around the different learning states, in contrast with their less creative peers.

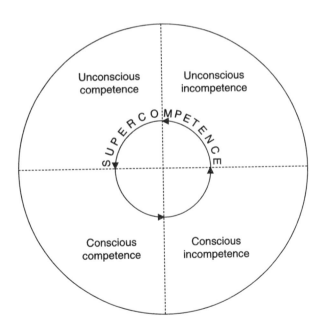

Figure 13.2 *The skills of conscious supercompetent practitioners*

9. SPEAK THE LANGUAGE OF THE POSITIVE

If only people could press the button in their heads that controls their amazing ability to visualize the future, and switch it from negative to positive, they would improve their creativity 1,000 per cent.

An observation to creativity course delegates

Commitment and flexibility of mind underlie a positive attitude in the creative personality. This positiveness is neither a blind optimism nor starry-eyed wishful thinking. It is a 'can do' view based on an assessment of events. It is speaking the language of the positive.

This positive spirit works on two levels. Firstly, it operates as a supporting attitude of mind when tackling a task. Secondly, it seems to work in an almost magnetic way in attracting other positive elements.

A positive supporting state of mind

Everyone has a high level of skill in being able to visualize the future. We can depict scenarios in incredible detail with a remarkable vividness capable of inducing intense reactions and feelings in the body. This ability is called worry.

Think for a moment about a potential concern, or the time you were faced with a possible problem; when you thought you had lost your wallet, or when your child had gone missing. These can lead to very intense experiences of anxiety and concern, when you envisage a whole range of possible misfortunes in lurid detail.

Does the average person engage, on a similar level, this ability to visualize potential scenarios for positive opportunities? The answer is 'no'. If only we *could* employ this talent for visualizing, but use it in the positive, it would significantly improve our ability to deal with embryonic activities. Too many people live their lives through F.E.A.R. – Forever Expecting Awful Results.

The creative person is often described as someone who is prepared to take risks. The opposite is true. Because they are able to visualize positively, they do not see possible weaknesses as major obstacles. Instead, they have established a concrete image of the potential of the embryonic idea, and therefore do not see the uncertainties as risky.

A positive self-belief is not a licence for arrogance. Rather, it is a

self-view that, come what may, you believe that what you are doing is right. During a crisis PR situation, back in 1991, when trying to save the Treats Ice Cream factory in Leeds from closure by its then parent group Unilever, a colleague said to me: 'Do you realize who you are taking on?' The reply was: 'Do they know who *they* are taking on?' Even though we were opposed to one of the major corporations in the world, a positive belief that we were going to succeed, no matter what the odds, was eventually proved right. This attitude is perhaps best summed up by the rock musician, Frank Zappa, in his autobiography *The Real Frank Zappa* (1989): 'Just because several million people think you're wrong, it doesn't mean they're right.'

This arrogance about your skills is not necessarily based on having an exceptionally high IQ, which is not a prerequisite for creativity. Indeed, it may inhibit the inner resources of the creative individual because the Red Light thinking modes of self-criticism are too rigid, and too dominant over your own Green Light thinking abilities. There are numerous instances of creative geniuses, such as Darwin and Einstein, who did not do well at school.

A positive self-belief also fuels the quality of curiosity in creative minds. This attitude is encapsulated as: 'I don't know what it is I'm going to find, but I'm sure it's going to be good.' There is a tendency for people to see the 10 per cent of the bad in an idea, and overlook the remaining 90 per cent that may offer some potential for added value. Mozart was apparently a pathological optimist. He even considered that his blindness in later life offered new opportunities.

The latest developments in sports psychology stress the importance of positive thinking in achieving outstanding performance. These views are equally valid in the world of creative public relations. A single negative thought can apparently bring about more than 100 biochemical changes in our body. The psychologists argue that if you do not control your thoughts, the negative thoughts are going to control you. One creative friend advised me to stay away from negative people who drain your energy – their influence, he argued, is 'psychotoxic'! We all know completely negative people who we are glad to get away from because at times they make us feel miserable or bring us down to their state of negative thinking.

A positive magnet to the world around you

Serendipity is the art of making happy and unexpected discoveries by accident. You will have had experiences of starting to look for something, and other things starting to fall into place. This is like the time a knitting yarn client wanted me to come up with a stunt for the 'Children in Need' charity appeal. Lo and behold, we discovered in the *Guinness Book of Records* that the woman who at the time held the record for being the fastest knitter in the world, Gwen Matthewman (a lovely lady), lived just down the road from us in Featherstone, West Yorkshire, and was available for a sponsored knit. Luck you might say; perhaps, but as Louis Pasteur observed: 'Chance favours the prepared mind.'

Now, you might say this is a bit of mumbo-jumbo, this arguing that positive things outside your control can be drawn to you. Yet one of the cleverest brains of all time, the great writer Goethe, reflected that when you start doing things, it acts as a trigger for attracting events completely beyond your influence. He observed:

> The moment one definitely commits oneself, then providence moves too. All sorts of things occur to help me, that would never otherwise have occurred. A whole stream of events issues from the decision, raising in one's favour all manner of unforeseen incidents and material assistance, which no man could have dreamed would have come his way. Whatever you can do or dream you can, begin it. Boldness has genius, power and magic in it. Begin it now.

The outstanding creative writer Tony Buzan has taken the concept of serendipity a stage further, with what he calls 'Goethendipity' (Buzan, 1994). He puts forward the idea that the people you meet, and the circumstances in which you find yourself, will relate incredibly closely to the power of your personal vision, the commitment you have to it, the persistence with which you pursue it, your appropriate practice of the brain principles, and the degree of your development of the other characteristics of genius. Now that's a positive thought for you.

10. REACH FOR THE STARS

Henry Moore, the sculptor, was apparently once chipping away at a block of stone and, when asked what he was doing, replied: 'There is a reclining nude inside, and I'm helping her to get out.'

A management legend from Castleford

A strong sense of personal vision is vital to the creative practitioner. 'Vision' means how you have made a goal, or series of goals, in your life so that they are as vivid in your mind, as clearly articulated, and as comprehensively understood as possible.

This sense of vision applies to yourself, in what you want to achieve with your life, and also the task you are working on. Think for a moment about your ambitions in life. Where do you see yourself in a year's time, or five years' time? Think about the next project you are about to work on. Is it going to be a run-of-the-mill piece of work, or do you have ambitions for it to be a major award-winning and recognized campaign? As the punk musician Captain Sensible once sang: 'If you don't have a dream, how are you gonna have a dream come true?'

Whether it is the future of your life, or the next press release, there is a quality threshold in operation with your vision. Leo Burnett, a legend of the American advertising scene, is quoted in David Ogilvy's *Advertising* (Ogilvy, 1987) as saying: 'When you reach for the stars, you may not quite get one, but you won't come up with a handful of mud either!' Consequently, if you do not have high hopes either for yourself or for the particular piece of work you are working on, how can you ever expect you or it to amount to anything?

Creative practitioners can translate the raw material of information and ideas into the medium of a public relations campaign. They can envisage the potential media coverage or results from an activity. An outstanding creative practitioner will not only share this experience, but also couple it with an ability to visualize it achieving even greater success.

Unfortunately, this ability to visualize outstandingly good results does have a downside: creative people, whether in public relations or other fields, are never satisfied. Woody Allen, the brilliant film director, does not like any of his films as he sees the flaws and shortcomings compared with his original concepts. The novelist Irish Murdoch said in a *Guardian* interview: 'I live with an

absolute continuous sense of failure. I am always defeated, always. Every book is the wreck of a perfect idea.' Terence Conran, the design guru, is credited with saying that he had 'never met a truly creative person who was happy and satisfied with life. They always worried about something, that something is not right with which they could improve the world'.

In dealing with this dissatisfaction, be encouraged by the philo- sophical response of the great jazz musician Duke Ellington, when told he had been ripped off by his agent. Asked why he was not angry, Duke replied: 'I'll just write another song.' It is the prospect of another 'song' – whether it is the next press release, or a major new campaign, or the next 10,000 words of a book like this – and the vision for the project that it is going to be the greatest thing ever invented that helps to reinvigorate the practitioner. It restores a sense of further purpose, and it enables the successful public relations practitioner to continue to be creative.

And one final tip. Set yourself 10 personal goals for the year ahead. Write them down and put the list in your desk drawer. In a year's time, you might be surprised how many of your goals you have either reached or are nearer to achieving.

AND 11. BREAK THE RULES, BE HAPPY AND HAVE FUN

Let's do it anyway.

Words of encouragement to a colleague

This is not the anarchist section of the book but, as George Bernard Shaw observed: 'The reasonable man adapts himself to the world. The unreasonable man adapts the world to him. Therefore, all progress depends on unreasonable men.'

By being creative, you are in the business of creating 'new'. To create new may often mean discarding, or abandoning, the old way of doing. This book has looked at how you need to be flexible, to think outside the box. How you may often be held back by what you perceive as the rules of a situation. Be prepared to grasp opportunities and stand up when required to say: 'I am prepared to break the rules of this situation.' Indeed, actually do something naughty – so long as it does not hurt anyone or contravene the

laws of the land. It can be a liberating experience and help fuel your creative drive.

You must enjoy your work. You can only be really good at what you love to do. Unless you find the whole process pleasurable – every part of it – you will not succeed. If you do not get that feeling in public relations, then maybe another career path may be best for you, in which you may be able to fulfil your creative potential. The management guru Stephen Covey talks of the need to have your fundamental beliefs in tune with what you are doing in life in order to be successful and happy.

Treat your life as a work of art – to give pleasure in the production of it, and pleasure to others as a result of your labours. Having fun is vital for the highly creative public relations practitioner. We only have one life; make the most of it. To echo the words of one of my dearest friends, Amanda Marsh: 'This is not a rehearsal.'

Remember the rules to be a more creative person:

Be uncomfortable.
Be a pig, a mule and Zebedee.
Have a positive anchor and be Robert Davy.
Overflow your jug.
Take your hunches to lunch.
Work, work – and work.
Be a professor of public relations and parlez PR
Is your escalator a stairway?
Speak the language of the positive.
Reach for the stars.
Break the rules, be happy and have fun.

SUMMARY

1. There is no one ingredient that makes individuals creative.
2. Creative people are characterized by self-belief, determination and hard work. They have mentors, consume large amounts of information or experience, trust their intuition, have high-quality job skills, and a flexible mind. Also, they are positive, with a strong personal vision, are prepared to redefine the rules, and enjoy their work.

3. As a creative individual you will disagree with at least one or more points in this book, or whole chapters, or even the whole book.

KEY WORDS FOR YOUR CREATIVITY VOCABULARY

- Commitment.
- 'Creative catalogues'.
- Flexible learning states.
- Fun.
- Janusian thinking.
- Outside the box.
- Positive anchors.
- Power hunches.
- Reframing.
- Role models.
- Serendipity.
- Surfing.
- Vision.
- Visualization.

14

Creating a creative culture

Person in charge of saying 'No'.
> *Sign that the comedian Kenny Everett once put on a*
> *BBC bureaucrat's office door*

Creativity does not just reside within individuals but is also influenced by, and manifests itself within, organizations. This chapter will look at how organizations can improve their overall creativity, manage creative individuals within the organization, and structure their creative resources.

THE 'CREATIVE CHALLENGE'

Just as individuals may vary in their respective creative talents, organizations will be characterized by their varying degrees of creative abilities. Most textbooks and studies on the subject of creativity and innovation focus on how the organization can be shaped to come up with more ideas. The task is to move the organization further up the creative–non-creative scale, as in Figure 14.1, in terms of generating ideas.

Non-creative ——————————————————————————————— **Creative**

Figure 14.1 *The creativity continuum*

As identified in Chapter 1, there are a number of so-called 'tribes' in public relations who, when it comes to creativity, are characterized either by dashing off into dottiness or only addressing the nuts and bolts of a situation. A common complaint about public relations consultancies in the UK is: 'You get some who are very good at coming up with ideas but are lousy at getting things done. There are others who cannot come up with ideas but are good at getting things done.'

A fundamental theme of this study into creativity is that the creative practitioner – either an individual or an organization – is focused on providing added value. The task facing managers is not just how the organization can generate more ideas and be more effective in its Green Light thinking skills but also how they can couple this with the necessary Red Light thinking skills of implementation in order to achieve added value. The challenge for public relations organizations is not just to position themselves across one dimension of a creative scale of generating ideas but rather, at the same time, to map out their position on a second scale, namely that of the ability to implement. This double-scale approach is represented in Figure 14.2. For the public relations organization, the 'Creative Challenge' (as I have called it) is to score highly on both scales.

By identifying their position within the Creative Challenge, managers can adopt a number of strategies for seeking greater added value from their creative resources, through:

- *achieving greater balance between generating ideas and acting upon them,* by developing the skills of their team, putting additional resource in time, people or facilities in the areas of the Creative Challenge that are weak;
- *developing a tandem operation* in which the missing or weak skills are outsourced in some way – for instance, an in-house department may use the services of a consultancy, or a public relations consultancy may use the services of a growing band of specialist creative consultancy services;

Figure 14.2 *The Creative Challenge: creativity and implementation in combination*

- *recognizing that their strengths lie in just one area of the Creative Challenge* and focusing on this particular quality.

Where does your organization sit within the Creative Challenge? Map out its position.

MANAGING CREATIVE INDIVIDUALS

In the same way that a manager may look at building on the organization's strengths and compensating for its weaknesses in the Creative Challenge, so that manager should actively manage individuals within the team in the same manner. The skilful manager builds around the strengths of the individual, and uses other members of the team with complementary skills to compensate for any imbalance. As a result, it is possible to achieve a balance between the Green Light thinking skills of coming up with ideas and Red Light thinking skills of implementation. Building teams by recognizing individuals' qualities may sound rather obvious but, sadly, it is a skill missing from too many managers in the profession.

Rather than moving into great detail about team building, you may be interested in one route (of profiling the individual components of a successful team) devised by R Meredith Belbin. Table 14.1 plots the different profiles considered necessary for a productive team, and particularly a creative organization. You do not

Table 14.1 *Belbin's team profiling*

Role of individual	Description of abilities
Plant	Creative, imaginative and often unorthodox; has an ability to solve difficult problems.
Resource manager	Extrovert, enthusiastic and communicative; explores opportunities and develops contacts.
Coordinator	Tends to be mature in attitude, confident and can be a good chairperson; clarifies goals, promotes decision making and delegates well.
Shaper	The doer – challenging and dynamic; thrives on pressure; has the drive and courage to overcome obstacles.
Monitor/evaluator	Sober, strategic and discerning; sees all options; tends to be an accurate judge of a situation.
Team worker	Cooperative, mild-mannered, perceptive and diplomatic; listening skills build relationships and avert friction; tends to calm the waters when tensions arise within a team.
Implementer	Disciplined, reliable, conservative, efficient; turns ideas into practical actions.
Completer	Painstaking, conscientious and can be anxious; searches out errors and omissions, yet will deliver on time.
Specialist	Single-minded, self-starting and dedicated; provides knowledge and skills in rare supply.

necessarily have to have a representative from each profile to be an effective team – indeed, many public relations operations are smaller than nine people. Nevertheless, the principle behind the theory – of the need to display, in some form, the characteristics detailed in each of the profiles – is still pertinent to a successful operation.

 What profiles do you think are represented in your team? Is there an imbalance or a shortage of particular skills?

When managing creative people, care should be taken in evaluating their work. Outstandingly creative work is a result of a high level of commitment. As a result, what creative people produce is not, in their eyes, just a piece of work; rather, it represents an extension of themselves – it is something that they have drawn from within themselves for the sake of their work. As a writer said to a friend who asked how difficult it was to write a book: 'Easy, you just sit in front of your computer and give blood.'

If a piece of creative work is in some way not up to scratch, as a manager, you should say what is good about it first. Never say: 'This is rubbish' (or worse), as the people concerned will take it personally. You are not just criticizing a piece of work but are, in their eyes, criticizing something that is a part of them. Always present your views positively and objectively. For example, you could say: 'Great idea, let's build upon it...', or 'Let us adapt it or make it work in this context', or 'How does this score against our client's needs?' It's important to coax your colleagues into challenging themselves. By being positive and objective, you keep the personal at bay, with analysis and rejection solely on factual grounds.

THE CHARACTERISTICS OF A CREATIVE ORGANIZATION

The skills, qualities and attitudes of the creative individual discussed in the previous chapter are mirrored by the characteristics of the creative organization. By understanding them, and considering how your organization relates to each facet, you can identify weaknesses – and then you can start to improve the performance of the organization.

The mirrored characteristics can be considered in line with the '10 rules' (plus the paradoxical eleven) listed in the previous chapter, as set out hereafter.

Be uncomfortable: encourage ideas

Public relations organizations are at an advantage, compared with those in other sectors, in being at the forefront of dealing with, and seeking to manage, new issues. In the nature of the work of the public relations organization, there can be a preponderance of short-term activities, with very short lead times, resulting in more opportunities to try something novel. This can create a greater willingness to accept new things.

Against this, however, are a number of significant conservative constraints to change. Many public relations initiatives are dependent on the co-operation of a third party, such as the media, in using a particular story, or on other parts of the organization's management in sanctioning an initiative. Practitioners may feel reluctant to expose themselves to ridicule, or apathy, by trying something new. Underlying all public relations activities is the need to avoid compromising the brand and values of the organization. This again can constrain the desire to try something new.

There is a tendency to regard creativity as a bolt-on function to apply either when the fancy takes a manager or in times of difficulty. For a creative organization, it is vital that the belief in creativity is instilled and supported at all management levels. The need to allow risks, supported by a collective acceptance of risk-taking and doing things in a new or different way, is paramount. This should be translated into a culture of openness.

The task of managers is to create an environment that encourages ideas from anywhere. Obviously, a system of openness runs contrary to an autocratic management style, which displays a reluctance to relinquish power and control. Without this toleration of discomfort – being open and permissive, encouraging each member of the team to participate – the potential for creativity is severely limited.

Be pigs, mules and Zebedees: make creativity a mindset

Creative organizations tend to be led from the top, with the senior manager having a belief in and commitment to creativity. As Graham Lancaster of Biss Lancaster observes: 'Creativity is a mindset, and a behavioural thing, rather than a short burst of energy. It needs top-down support, from the Chief Executive

Officer level downwards, to create structures and a culture in which innovation and creativity take place, where people are encouraged to be proactive in problem solving.' Without this commitment, successful creative activity often occurs *despite* the system rather than because of it.

Paul Carroll, formerly of Communique, is typical of creative leaders in his reaction to requests from colleagues for ideas:

> Whenever somebody in the office puts an e-mail out – and you might get two or three a week – asking if anybody has got any ideas or suggestions on how we can do this, or get this story, I always respond. It's almost a competitive thing. I pride myself that with any e-mail like that, I want to answer it. I am like a big kid. I want my idea to be the one that the client uses.

A desire to achieve is fundamental. A 'can do' culture will encourage the acceptance of new ideas and concepts, as opposed to a negative environment in which new ideas are met with resistance.

Creativity is recognized as a process to be used day in and day out, not a one-off event to be scheduled in times of trouble. Today's great companies eat creativity, sleep creativity, think creativity. M Douglas Ivester, President of the Coca-Cola Company, is quoted in John Kao's *Jamming* (Kao, 1996) as stating:

> You need to make creativity the norm and the lack of creativity the exception, as opposed to trying to take a company and say, 'Well, we're going to be creative this week.' You will be creative that week, but it will be totally irrelevant. It's important to establish an aspiration of creativity. If you go to any sort of meeting here, whether it's finance or marketing or technical, that aspiration, that expectation, is going to pop out. It'll just overwhelm you. That's what's inside people's heads. And it's what we preach to them.

Fundamentally, an organization's behaviour has to reflect the value it places on creativity. Also, its leadership must craft a meaningful challenge in order for its team to be creative, and not use the concept of creativity as an end in itself.

Determination and persistence are the great unsung heroes of creativity, both for the individual and the organization. The world is full of unsuccessful men and women of talent. Geniuses will often go unrewarded. It is persistence and determination

by individuals and their organizations that mark out the really creative groups. Coca-Cola, according to M Douglas Ivester, demonstrates this by producing a climate of creativity through ceaseless reinforcement.

The leading creative public relations organizations similarly match this drive, recognizing that creativity is a process that they need in order to orchestrate 1,001 small acts and behaviours. Whether it is the way the phone is answered or the way a major promotional campaign is delivered, these functions add up to make the creative organization what it is.

Have positive anchors for the team and have Robert Davy as MD: create creative space

Most founders of creative public relations companies tend to be high on personal charisma and have the determination to develop the business 'their way'. In these circumstances, the leader of an organization tends to serve both as a role model and a mentor to the teams. In other instances, an outside figure may be identified as a suitable role model or mentor.

The use of anchoring, the technique of eliciting a positive feeling to support the creative spirit, can be used by organizations in a physical sense, by providing a special area or space that is conducive to creative activities. This type of creative space can be a formal 'Open Space', such as a room dedicated to creative thoughts, with special furnishings or a distinctive ambience to mark it out from normal rooms. Alternatively, it may be an informal area – in large organizations, greater creativity is often the result of encounters on stairways or at the photocopy machine, where staff happen to meet, rather than in formal settings.

A dedicated Open Space can encourage abandonment of anxieties and stimulate an openness to new ideas and approaches. When the great jazz musician Charlie Parker needed to work out new musical concepts, he would withdraw and, as he put it, 'go to the woodshed' to look for new ideas and inspiration. Similarly, organizations may have their own formal or informal 'woodshed' to serve as a venue that encourages creativity.

Alternatively, practitioners may use a variety of props to serve as a positive anchor, such as alcohol at brainstorming events. Here, it is not so much the intoxicating qualities of the beverages that encourage creativity; rather it is more a question of their symbolic

value – by signalling that we are doing something different as a group, we are approaching things in different ways, we are breaking our normal rules. A similar effect is achieved in a technique used by one consultancy where a tennis ball is thrown between members of the group as they come up with an idea in a brainstorm.

Overflow each individual's jug: stimulate your staff

The creative organization is not a one-hit wonder, just producing an outstanding idea and then sitting back to enjoy the benefits of its inspiration. It is constantly looking to create new ideas, and to be innovative by adopting or adapting the ideas produced by third parties. Winning companies constantly introduce new and differentiated products and services for their clients.

This state of affairs can only be truly achieved by creating a work environment that encourages individuals to absorb and draw in inspiration from the widest range of stimuli. When Lou Gerstner took over IBM, he ordered 50,000 subscriptions to *Wired* magazine to encourage his new team to look beyond conventional sources of information. Conversely, I knew someone who once worked at a consultancy that only took in one newspaper a day for its staff to read; needless to say, that person did not stay there long.

The creative public relations department or consultancy has to look at every way of stimulating its people, whether through information, variety of experiences, contact with outside people, or variety in work settings. The creative organization will recognize that good ideas come from anywhere, and will be looking to encourage all levels of the group to participate, while in turn contributing to their individual development.

Take your hunches to lunch: have confidence in your people

The classic new product story of the Sony Walkman illustrates the benefits of trusting hunches. When the idea was first mooted, it was claimed that it could not be done, nor would it sell. Subsequent events proved otherwise.

Respect for the hunch is another feature of the creative organization. It is unrealistic to expect an organization to be tolerant of supporting their individual team members' hunches unless the other elements – belief in and commitment to creativity – are already established characteristics. The effective harnessing of hunches can only be put into practice where there is confidence that the team members possess the necessary professional skills and knowledge to provide a suitable seed-bed that will nurture and develop the 'power hunch'.

Work: be supportive

Outstanding creative organizations do not just play at creativity. They maintain a balance between Green Light and Red Light thinking skills. It is not sufficient just to have ideas. Douglas Adams, in his series *A Hitchhiker's Guide to the Galaxy*, hilariously describes a planet made up of useless people, who are very good at coming up with new ideas but who have few practical skills, in contrast to the planet of useful people who are good at doing things. An outstandingly creative organization cannot exist in a world of useless people.

The balance between ideas and integration is achieved by having structures and cultures in place that support both areas of thinking. One all-too-common mistake is to confuse the word 'creativity' with 'activity'. To shape a culture in which creativity flourishes, there is a need to build it into systems that enable it to be lived every day.

An idea of this in everyday behaviour is when a colleague has an idea that may require your time and attention. Think twice before replying: 'Can you write me a note, or a report on it.' By doing this, you are putting in place a bureaucratic obstacle, and are saying in effect: 'I'm too busy and not prepared to give you the necessary support', instead of genuinely facilitating the creativity of a fellow team member. Providing the necessary support to enable colleagues to be creative is hard work – and there is no substitute for it.

Be professors of PR: encourage learning

Whether it is in the creative dimensions or any other aspect of public relations work, an organization is only as good as its

people. Effective creative skills can only be achieved through extensive, well-organized professional knowledge. This will give the organization an edge in its creativity and an ability to come up with creative solutions.

A learning culture, with an emphasis on team members acquiring and developing professional skills, is fundamental to nurturing a creative organization. Also, an organization committed to being at the cutting edge of its profession is likely to be at the forefront of new ideas and opportunities, to provide it with a further competitive edge.

Tolerate the escalators being stairways: have a dual perspective

Sir Peter Ustinov, in his autobiography *Dear Me* (1977), recalls his school report, which read: 'He shows originality, which must be curbed at all costs.' This is a comment sadly reflected in the attitudes of too many organizations.

Flexibility of thought is a vital requisite of the creative group. It harnesses the individual talents of its members and it provides the necessary group support and assistance to enable ideas to develop and achieve their full potential. A flexible culture is required for creative organizations on two levels.

Firstly, in its management of its people it needs to give exceptional people exceptional boundaries within which to operate. The creative organization has to be flexible to permit Green Light thinking and to allow its team members sufficient scope to operate and flourish. Rigid bureaucracies are not conducive to creativity. The organizational structure has to be flexible to meet, and adapt to, new situations and circumstances.

Secondly, the creative organization needs to be able to work in a number of different perspectives. On one, it will be seeking to develop and extend its professional expertise, yet on another it should be able to maintain a state of beginner's mind so as to enable it to see potential opportunities and alternatives. This dual perspective is essential if the organization is to have a handle on the detail of its work and to steer it to develop new strategies and game plans.

Speak the common language of the positive, tolerate failures and drive out fear

A key motivation behind creative organizations is the positive desire to deliver products and services that exceed customers' expectations by offering significant added value. The creative organization is based on a positive premise that it looks continually to improve its performance and examine every aspect of its operation in order to identify any further opportunities for added value.

A positive attitude underpins the culture of a creative organization in providing tolerance of failure. It will look at the positives to be drawn from any experience, and at the potential for new opportunities to counterbalance any setbacks. A positive spirit will also work to drive out fear from the organization, because frightened people can neither work well, nor be empowered to generate new creative ideas. As Alan Preece of the University of East Anglia observed when interviewed:

> The best way of getting anything out of people, not just in creativity, is to give them real latitude to fail. But to fail honestly from their own endeavours, having worked hard to try to make it succeed. Because there are great lessons to be learnt in failure. You have to create an environment in which people are allowed to think the impossible. You have to protect them from criticism from other parts of the organization, which might feel quite jealous, or that their toes are being trodden on. And if you're responsible for people, to an extent you have to have broad shoulders and bear the brunt of the flak when things go wrong.

Reach for the stars: have a mission

The creative organization does not just value good ideas but puts them on a pedestal to admire, respect and serve as a stimulus for further creative effort. The Department of Trade and Industry, in a recent study, notes how successful companies are led by visionary, enthusiastic champions of change. Likewise, the creative organization embarks upon an exploration that is never finished, a journey that never ends. As success is a state of mind rather than a destination, so the sense of vision, shared through every layer of the creative organization, is one of constantly getting ahead rather than of arriving.

The creative organization needs clear leadership and an overall shared vision. It has a creed that there are no unmotivated or uninnovative people at work, only poor managers failing to harness their teams' potential. The organization's vision is the vital magnet available to draw out the potential of individual team members to the aspirations of the group. The task of managers is not to put creativity into their teams, but to draw it out, for the creativity is already there.

The other characteristics identified in this chapter on creative organizations serve as mechanisms to facilitate this drawing out of creative talent. Without a shared vision the team's energies can be dissipated, or go off at a tangent.

In the same way that Woody Allen is apparently never happy with his films, the managers of the creative organization are never happy with the end product. On the surface this may be seen as a result of competition from others, but ultimately the greatest competition they face is themselves. By having a strong sense of vision, the managers not only drive the organization forward but are also the motor for keeping it in constant motion.

Break the rules and have fun – and mean it

Many of us can relate to the comment attributed to the rocket scientist Werner von Braun, when he said: 'We can lick gravity, but sometimes the paperwork is overwhelming.' To counter the deadening hand of bureaucracy, some organizations have gone as far as adopting a corporate edict along the lines of: 'Every rule here can be challenged, except this one.'

The latest fashion in corporate management-speak is for companies to adopt an ethos of having fun at work. This recognizes the fact that people spend most of their lives at their workplace, and the committed creative organization will ask what can be done to make the time of its employees as fulfilling and enjoyable as possible. The reality of most organizations' efforts to this end is, however, that their corporate behaviours fail to live up to their glib aspirations.

Any practitioner wanting to see an example of a public relations organization successfully integrating the fun elements into its everyday work is recommended to visit the website of Oak Ridge Public Relations, based in Cupertino, California. The firm, run by husband-and-wife team Tom and Kathy Keenan, practises what is

preaches. Whether it is including a fun *nom de plume* on each of its business cards, or providing a special room on site for their staff's children, full of toys, games and educational material, Oak Ridge is proving that it is possible to work hard and play hard without just posturing on this issue. It is also a very successful company.

THE CREATIVE DIRECTOR – TO HAVE OR HAVE NOT?

In providing a structure for creativity within public relations organizations, should there be a role comparable to that of the creative director in an advertising agency? Here would be a person who, at the very least, would be the champion of creativity, or have a specific line function to produce creative ideas. The idea of a similar role within public relations companies provokes a mixed response among practitioners.

Graham Lancaster of Biss Lancaster argues against the idea. He said when interviewed: 'I feel quite strongly about that. I think that it is wrong. It suggests that it's someone else's job, like there's a creative lightning conductor that you can departmentalize or compartmentalize into someone else's responsibility. It's entirely counterintuitive to the way I think.'

Steve Gebbett of Charles Barker is more equivocal. Speaking from first-hand experience of the role, he said:

> I was named as one of the only two Creative Directors in Britain in the 1980s and, to this day, find myself in a unique position in PR consultancy. But as a Creative Director, the first thing is to create a catalyst by which you can help colleagues to be creative themselves, because of course to be creative is in no one person's gift. It does have to be, if you like, learnt and developed among all practitioners. That really is the central role of the Creative Director, to ensure that creativity is seen as a fundamental part of the public relations approach.

Paul Carroll is positive towards the idea in one respect. He feels that the advantages of such a position lie in its marketing benefits rather than as a means of producing higher-value creativity:

Maybe I'm a bit too old-fashioned or maybe too cynical. I know that some consultancies have started to introduce that role or department. I don't think those people are going to be more creative than others. Where they might possibly score is that they have put a brass plaque on that door saying 'Creativity and genius contained within'. From a marketing point of view it's a good ploy, but it could be faddish, and that's the danger in my opinion. However, the title may also help to heighten the clients' expectations. It probably also increases the likelihood that clients will listen, and maybe they have found one way of selling there. We all know in this game about the Emperor's new clothes; by branding it 'creativity', their ideas might be recognized as great ideas even if they're not.

On balance, Alan Preece is dismissive of the role:

I don't think it is necessary. It depends on the nature of the organization itself. I think that some creative directors can perform some roles. They can set tone and direction, which is a way of guiding the spirit of the organization. They could also add value through their experience, where they can oil the wheels of creativity in action, so they can bring people together. At their very best, I guess, they can inspire the impossible among people, particularly if they are able to have demonstrated that they have been there and done it themselves. Fundamentally, though, individual practitioners have to be their own creative directors.

This last point is a view echoed by Gordon Forbes of Ptarmigan, when he turns the issue on its head by saying: 'I think that every PR person should be a creative person. We shouldn't be called PR consultants. We should all be called creative consultants, because that's what we are doing, really.'

The arguments for having the post of creative director thus rest on it providing a focus for the creative element within a company and serving as standard-bearer for the cause of creativity. For many consultancies, built up around a charismatic creative individual, as they get bigger, the direct influence of the founder may become diluted. Having someone else as creative director can provide a further focus for the issue of creativity. Informally, most organizations already have someone who is looked upon as having extra ability for 'coming up with ideas'. Bestowing the title of Creative Director merely formalizes an existing specialism.

Having someone with the title of Creative Director does give greater status to the selling of the idea of creativity and offers

added weight to that part of the service being sold. Also, many clients are used to the structure of advertising agencies in which there is someone with the specific title of Creative Director, and such clients would perhaps be more comfortable with a corresponding position in their public relations consultancy.

The arguments against having a creative director rest on the fundamental issue that everyone working on a public relations campaign has a responsibility – in some way or another – for being creative and managing the creative dimension in his or her work. The reality of creativity, from my own experience, is that the best ideas come while working on an issue, in the Integration stage of the creative process, rather than made to order away from the 'coalface' of the situation. Those working day in and day out on a task will have more information and a better understanding of the realities of a potential idea; they will be better placed to identify the real problems that need solving.

Divorcing the creation of ideas from their subsequent execution gives rise to the potential danger of the 'not invented here' syndrome; there is less of a feeling of ownership of the problem from those working on the project if the ideas have come from elsewhere. In order for creativity to be successful, the team must be committed to seeing an idea through, to overcoming obstacles, and to ensuring that what emerges is worthy of the original idea. This determination to succeed is likely to be keenly possessed by those whose idea it is in the first place.

Operationally, there could be dangers of ego, of creative directors having their head in the clouds, with a tendency to 'dash off into dottiness' to justify their position, rather than coolly analyse what added value is required. Furthermore, there could be an insecurity on the part of talented consultancy staff who do not want to be divorced from direct contact or relationships with clients. Public relations consultancies also tend to have a greater number of clients per head of staff than their counterparts in an advertising agency, making it difficult to recreate the creative director role.

With greater specialization and growth in the size of the larger consultancies, the potential use of creative directors is likely to become more widespread. However, creating hundreds of job titles across the country does not provide a magic wand for the industry to instantly improve its creative abilities. Creativity will still be a fundamental skill for every practitioner to employ, and a challenge for organizations to manage in their employees.

 Would your organization benefit from someone having the job title of Creative Director?

SUMMARY

1. The Creative Challenge for organizations is to balance the ability to generate ideas with the skills for making them work.
2. There is no one ingredient that characterizes the creative organization.
3. Managers should look to build teams around the strengths of their individual members.
4. No one person in an organization can be solely responsible for being creative. The job of creative director can be useful as a catalyst for the creative function and in the selling of ideas. However, the idea also has a number of disadvantages.

KEY WORDS FOR YOUR CREATIVITY VOCABULARY

- Creative challenge.
- Creative space.

15

The ethics of creativity: lies, damned lies and impropaganda

Public relations is a broad church; within it there are some who are more ecumenical with the truth than others.

Comment from a leading PR practitioner

This book has examined how creativity – combining different elements to provide added value – can be used by practitioners, and the assumption is that the different elements are factually correct. Sometimes, however, individual publicists have used the euphemism of 'creative licence' with a degree of flexibility in their handling of the facts available to them in order to produce added value, particularly in achieving media coverage.

DEALING WITH 'IMPROPAGANDA'

A disregard for facts in a communication, or even a lack of facts in

a situation, or the manipulation of the objective focus in any communication, can be labelled 'impropaganda'. Many practitioners may be dismissive of this type of publicity, in which fundamental principles of truth are felt to have been compromised. However, it is essential, in order to gain a full understanding of the subject of creativity in public relations, to study this area of work. It is only by examining this subject that we can then distinguish between the work of the opportunistic publicist and the genuine public relations practitioner.

It is important to establish a context within which public relations practitioners can operate. The Chartered Institute of Public Relations in its Code of Conduct sets down standards for practitioners. Its extensive Code covers a wide range of issues relating to honesty, and specifically states:

> Members of the Institute of Public Relations agree to: 'Maintain the highest standards of professional endeavour, integrity, confidentiality, financial propriety and personal conduct; Deal honestly and fairly in business with employers, employees, clients, fellow professionals, other professions and the public... Fundamental to good public relations practice are: Honest and responsible regard for the public interest; Checking the reliability and accuracy of information before dissemination; Never knowingly misleading clients, employers, employees, colleagues and fellow professionals about the nature of representation or what can be competently delivered and achieved.

The Code is not a piece of window dressing; members have a positive duty to observe its guidelines, which are upheld through the work of the Chartered Institute's Professional Practices Committee.

Much public relations work is concerned with media relations, where practitioners are a vital conduit of information to journalists. The great editor of the *Guardian* newspaper, C P Scott, once wrote that 'facts are sacred'. Yet this creed is undermined by three features of journalistic life: the speed of obtaining news and its subsequent dissemination; external controls that influence what information can and cannot be used; and cynicism among sections of the media.

Speed of dissemination

News, by definition, is telling people something new. The need to get the details before others do is paramount for news organizations in a competitive environment. In most embryonic news stories, the full facts will not be known. The perceived reality may contain a number of incontrovertible facts that can be substantiated; these may also be surrounded by layers of half-emerged facts and truths; and other details may take some time to crystallize into facts.

Journalists need to know quickly the details of the story and what is known about the situation they are reporting. They are most likely to have had limited prior knowledge about the situation, its background and the people involved – and certainly very limited time to make an assessment. As a result of this haste to tell the wider world, what will pass as news – even with the most respected of medium – will contain a mixture of facts, half-facts presented as facts, and speculation about other half-facts or details that will emerge later.

News gathering can only function effectively if there is a tolerance among journalists of which are being described as half-facts. News broadcasts will be considerably neutered if they have to wait for total substantiation of every detail in the story before relaying it to the public. In its Code of Practice for journalists, issued in 1998, the Guild of Editors lays emphasis on accuracy in reporting but does not specifically mention the word 'truth', and the Code contains only one reference to 'fact', in the context of separating fact from comment or conjecture.

In many instances, the public relations practitioner can be involved in situations where there is no intention to lie or deceive, but a story is run based on the best knowledge available at the time yet still essentially containing half-facts. Two examples from my working life as a former press officer with a water authority may demonstrate how half-facts were used by the media in their coverage of stories.

Around 20 skeletons were found during the construction of a flood defence scheme on the banks of the River Ouse in Yorkshire. They had evidently been there for centuries, but who were they and why were they buried in this remote spot? These were the questions posed by curious journalists. Immediately – and I do not know precisely where the theory came from – the comment

was made that they could have been Viking warriors buried as their comrades set sail back to Scandinavia after a raiding visit. This tale of Viking warriors caught the imagination of the media and national coverage followed, with television news showing various illustrations of warring Vikings. Yet no one had definite proof of this angle, only that the skeletons were found at a specific location. There was no evidence of archaeological remains or carbon dating of the bones, only the conjecture about who would bury a dozen people in a remote spot by a river in an area that had suffered from the raids of Vikings. A month later, there was little media coverage of the announcement that the skeletons were, in fact, the remains of a 17th-century plague pit.

The second example was during a spate of very cold weather, with ice and snow covering the ground, when there was a problem with the underwater outlet pipe to a reservoir in Halifax being blocked and interrupting supplies. The reporter got in touch and asked the water authority: 'What is causing the blockage?' The response given was that until the weather improved, the authority could not get underwater divers down to investigate and identify precisely what was causing the problem. Given the cold weather, it could have been ice. The reporter then remarked, 'So it could be a large block of ice blocking the pipe – almost like a mini iceberg?' The next day a story appeared of 'Mini iceberg stopping water to people's homes'. Several days later, divers found the cause of the blockage, which was a number of plastic bags – probably blown from nearby allotments – and certainly not a mini iceberg. This discovery did not receive any media coverage.

Information control

Both journalists and public relations practitioners work under a number of external controls, which can influence or dictate what information can or cannot be used. Laws of the land, such as those relating to libel or against incitement, coupled with security restrictions placed on certain items of information, can influence what is known in the public domain as 'the truth'. Prevailing values within our society can also proscribe what is said or not said. Organizations may have their reasons for limiting, or controlling, what information is issued to the public. Consequently, journalists find that often they cannot freely write or broadcast what

they know are the full facts. Similarly, public relations practitioners may be in situations where the information they issue is restricted or controlled in some way.

The cynical approach

Another aspect influencing media coverage is cynicism among a minority of individual journalists and certain sections of the media. This manifests itself in an attitude of 'not letting the facts get in the way of a good story'. Oscar Wilde observed: 'Lying for the sake of a monthly salary is, of course, well known in Fleet Street', while Mark Twain facetiously commented: 'Get your facts first, and then you are free to distort them as much as you please.'

This viewpoint is not intended to be a swipe at, or a damnation of, every journalist or media outlet. Nonetheless, there is a value system among a minority of journalists, and sections of the media, that has been labelled 'tabloid values', meaning that the facts are expendable or can be overlooked so as to avoid compromising the merits of a particular story.

Avoiding the pitfalls

In establishing how information is to be presented to the target audience, we also need to take into account the inherent character-istics of the creative practitioner. In Chapter 11, flexibility of thought was identified as one of the key traits of the creative person: the ability to run with what may only be partial truths, or half-emerged facts. Good practitioners have a toleration of oper-ating and working with the embryo of a fact rather than waiting for it to emerge as a piece of information that can be 100 per cent corroborated.

Edward L Bernays, one of the founding fathers of public rela-tions and author of *Propaganda*, written in 1928, defined the term 'impropaganda' as 'using propaganda techniques not in accor-dance with good sense, good faith, or good morals... using methods not consistent with the American pattern of behaviour based on Judeo-Christian ethics'. As this was written over 70 years ago, there is now a pressing need for a more specific definition in order to provide greater understanding and guidance for prac-tising in public relations.

The acts that, according to Bernays, are 'not in accordance with

good sense' can instead be specifically labelled 'shock PR' or 'punk PR'. The originator of the propaganda technique is seeking to create added value by going beyond what is regarded as mainstream 'good taste'. An activity described as 'a public relations exercise' – to cover a situation of communication with no substance within it – can more accurately be described as a 'pseudo-relations' exercise.

A more contemporary definition of 'impropaganda' proposed by the author is one wherein 'impropaganda goes beyond the controlled honesty inherent in public relations practice. It is a publicity act or media story that uses a flexibility with the facts and half-facts of a situation, or a manipulation of the objective focus in managing communications, to seek short-term added value for the promotion of a particular message or image. It is sustained by a shared value between the communicator and the audience' (or more simply, 'an untruth that both parties are happy to go along with'). The reference to 'controlled honesty' may seem a contrived effort to provide validity or justification for an act combining elements not wholly based on fact. Yet it is a fundamental distinction that separates public relations practice from impropaganda and outright lying.

When, even in legitimate public relations or journalistic activities, there may be external controls preventing full release of the potential information, there is a need to operate according to a system of values shared by the communicator and the recipient. Where 'impropaganda' is different from 'shock PR' or 'punk PR' or lying is where is it undertaken with either the cooperation or collusion of the medium – or, at the very least, operating within some form of shared values. The fundamental basis of this shared value is the mutual expediency between a communicator and the target audience. In the example of a news piece, through using 'impropaganda' in the telling of a particular story, a journalist and the medium gain in having an item, which under the guise of news may at least in some way entertain or satisfy the medium's audience. The publicist or press agent pursuing this line of action may obtain added value in the short term at least, by communicating certain messages or images contained within the story.

In the long term, however, the credibility of both the organization and its messenger may be compromised if it is seen to be lying or appears to be untrustworthy, and this lack of credibility may subsequently outweigh any short-term gain. It may also

compromise the standing and status of public relations practitioners – hence the Chartered Institute of Public Relations' determination in defining and upholding its Code of Conduct. Any member may be subject to action if a formal complaint against him or her is upheld by the Institute's Professional Practices Disciplinary Committee.

THE CREATIVE USE OF 'IMPROPAGANDA'

The creative use of 'impropaganda' in publicity and promotional work has been used for a number of specific functions, as set out below.

Shaping the facts: that's entertainment

By shaping the facts (or lack of facts) in a situation, added value can be gained in areas of work associated with public relations such as media relations, albeit in the short term. This may take the form of manipulating what can be called the face value of a situation. Here are two examples from the work of Mark Borkowski and Max Clifford.

Mark Borkowski describes a stunt he used to launch Oranjeboom, a lager drink, by using Dutch imagery in its branding:

> We planned the idea of a big 48-sheet poster with a press launch. The poster contained various words that were a form of pretend Dutch. This in itself would have not been inspiring or likely to get much media coverage. However, the night before the photocall, we arranged to have the poster spray-painted to give the impression that a vandal had been at work. As a result of this painting, various words were covered by the spray paint to leave only the (previously unconnected) letters making up a slang word for canine testicles.
>
> We got on the phone to journalists during the morning of the photocall to tell them it was cancelled because the poster had been defaced and we cannot have you there because of its rude content. Of course, people then wanted to cover it, saying how terrible it was. But they bought it.

Max Clifford, the well-known public relations entrepreneur, describes how he handled a major star who had an image of being a sex symbol but in real life was gay. Had the celebrity's sexual

orientation become known to the public, his career would have been ruined. Max dealt with this by contriving the facts. He recalled:

> So you create romances. You create a relationship with a stunning-looking woman, or a series of stunning-looking women, some of whom go to the papers and talk about their wild nights of passion with such and such. It does his career nothing but good. It dispels rumours that might be circulating. It means he becomes bigger and bigger box office, but there is no reality to it. That's creative. It solves the problem.

Shaping the facts: this is war

Outside the world of entertainment, shaping the facts may be justified by some publicists in situations where they feel the end justifies the means. Charity or campaign groups at the fringe of mainstream society may take risks if they feel this is the only way that they can advance their particular cause.

In the United States, it is reported that a number of campaigns of a dubious nature, pseudo grass roots community organizations, without any genuine or legitimate constituency, have been created in order to provide a front for promoting various causes. The inherent lack of legitimacy of these front organizations has led to them being dubbed 'Astroturf groups'.

In my own career, I was handling a campaign in 1991 when the future of a Leeds-based company, Treats Ice Cream, and the jobs of its 350 staff were at risk from a proposed closure by its then parent company, Walls, part of Unilever (see Chapter 9). There was concern that the parent company did not want to let another competitor emerge on the scene. We had to run a campaign with no resources and no official spokespeople to present the case that Treats had a future if a management buy-out were to go ahead. Because of the circumstances, the managers themselves were not allowed to make any public statement in support of their efforts. Our key point of leverage was to try and publicly embarrass Unilever into allowing the buy-out to go ahead.

Despite successfully getting the case aired, time was against us. We recognized that we had to have one last major push, as a final desperate measure to try to force Unilever's hand. A press conference was arranged, with the support of Leeds City Council, which provided the city's Civic Hall as a venue. It was announced that a

major advertising campaign was due to appear in the *Financial Times* and other quality publications, with a hard-hitting full-page advertisement that would attempt publicly to shame Unilever and say that time was running out. The conference received widespread exposure, with the advert copied by various newspapers and even on television. Yet, at the time, we had no money at all to run the advertisements as threatened. By using a tactic of bluff, significant editorial coverage was obtained, and it proved to be successful because shortly afterwards agreement was reached for a management buy-out, which saved the company and its 350 jobs.

Ironically, elsewhere in this book the term 'Goethendipity' has been used to describe occasions when, if you start something, other things quite unrelated move in to help it happen. In this instance, a senior officer at Leeds City Council came to me at the end of the press conference and said: 'Can we make a major contribution to fund the advertising campaign?'

Nonetheless, the decision to make flexible use of the facts, or what has subsequently been labelled 'impropaganda', did provide massive added value. Under the Chartered Institute of Public Relations' Code of Conduct, Clause 2.1, a 'member shall conduct his or her professional activities with proper regard to the public interest'. At the time, the public interest of saving the 350 jobs and guaranteeing the future well-being of employees was used to justify the actions.

Shaping the objectivity of a situation

Communicators have the ability to manage the available facts and information, not just in the extent to which they broadcast them but also in the way they define, or attempt to define, the focus of a situation. Although every constituent fact in a story may be 100 per cent corroborated, the prominence and emphasis given to certain facts is an element that can be managed and creatively used to provide added value. This can be done in three ways:

1. inflate the significance of a small part of the situation;
2. expand the context within which the event or development may be seen; and
3. mask or obscure the situation with a distraction.

Two examples, again from my days as a water industry press

officer during the 1980s, may illustrate how the objective focus may be manipulated.

We once received a call from an area office of the Water Authority, which went something like: 'Someone said we should give you a ring as we are closing a depot in North Yorkshire later this week and there might be some press interest.' Initially annoyed that we had not been contacted earlier, we tried to evaluate the negative impact of the situation and the resulting potential media interest, including whether any staff were being made redundant. 'There's only one person who is leaving, and that's our old tea lady who is over 80 years old and cannot travel to the new depot', said the caller.

Rather than put out a negative story about the rationalization of depots and a possible negative impact on service levels in the area, another angle was quickly identified; it was a marginal fact in the scheme of things, but it had good media potential as a human interest story. A news release was issued with the headline, 'Britain's oldest tea lady to retire' and a photocall was hastily arranged, at which she received a gift from grateful staff. The story received national and even international coverage. Yet none of the media had picked up on the reasons behind the tea lady's retirement and the potential ramifications for services and consumers, although these facts were included, albeit at the bottom of the release, after the human interest angle was fleshed out as much as possible.

On another occasion, the Water Authority carried out a major market research survey on the attitude of anglers to the Authority and the level of services provided for them. The findings were bad news for the Authority, containing very negative ratings and damning comments. However, we noticed one small fact in the survey: that one in three anglers went fishing accompanied by his wife.

Instead of focusing on the core of the report and its very negative findings, we issued the report and an accompanying news release with the intro that: 'One in three anglers admit to taking their wives with them when they go fishing.' The story led to national coverage with headlines like 'Her outdoors'. Even though the release said that full details of the survey were in the accompanying copy of the market research report, no one picked up on its findings because the journalists were content to use the spoon-fed, gimmicky news story.

The art of 'spin doctoring', of so-called media manipulation, has received significant public attention, but very little analysis. If it is defined as altering the objectivity of a situation (by using one of the three ways described earlier of shifting the objective focus of a story) creativity can be employed in: securing added value by effectively inflating a minor detail; or successfully going 'outside the box' of how a situation was initially perceived, to place it in a larger context. Finally, the creative 'spin doctor' may identify a new activity or issue that can be brought into place to provide a distraction to mask or obscure a point of concern.

The act of 'spinning', where the objectivity of a situation is altered, could be claimed to be a form of 'impropaganda'. The objectivity and focus of a situation are in themselves facts in the communication.

Alternatively, this management of the context of information could be argued as a legitimate tactic in public relations practice. Practitioners may feel it is valid to present their case, rather like a barrister, in the best possible light. The legal advocate analogy is, however, flawed; it ignores the long-term context of public relations work. A practitioner may win a one-off battle. Yet, unlike the legal advocate who walks away from a trial never having to put forward another case to the same jury, the public relations professional has to live day in and day out with the jury. Organizations, through the public relations function, have to present their case on a number of issues to the same groups of people who, in turn, will be passing judgement on them. If an organization seeks unscrupulously to win one argument, it will eventually be found out – to its cost when subsequently receiving a hearing on its further activities.

The extent to which practitioners have been creative with the focus of the situation, and how far they have practised a form of 'impropaganda', are subjects for further debate within the industry.

In her book *Ethics in Public Relations* (Parsons, 2004) Patricia J Parsons challenges the call I have made to extend the profession's vocabulary rather than be constrained by black-and-white definitions of 'lying' and 'truth'. This is interpreted by her as seeking:

> to avoid the public perception that we are lying. There is, I believe, cause to worry when we consider creating our own vocabulary, presumably with meanings that we as a profession create for the

purpose of avoiding the label of 'liar'. This is the kind of slippery slope that needs to be carefully considered before taking that first step.

This misses the fundamental point that existing definitions of emotive words such as 'liar' are too broad or imprecise. In reality, they become unwieldy and open to exploitation. If our language had a wider range of precisely defined words such as 'inflagate' – to inflate the significance of something; 'subligate' – to minimize the significance and subsume within its wider context; 'obstricate' – to use another object to cover up; 'altruisticlie' – to create a lie to protect a public good; these words or something similar would make a positive contribution to facilitating greater understanding.

Having an expanded vocabulary, of words with more precise meanings, could encourage more intelligent debate and create a more sophisticated understanding of the issues surrounding what is 'true', and what is a 'lie'. Rather than being a slippery downward slope it could mark as an upward, solid slope out of a quagmire of ambiguity or sloppy thinking surrounding so-called black-and-white definitions of telling the truth.

Before you decide that the idea of creating new words is too far fetched, it's worth mentioning that a new word – 'truthiness' – is gaining increasing currency. It was a term coined by television satirist Steve Colbert and can be defined as 'a story that you wish to be true but that does not correspond to reality'. The website www.greencomms.com gives an example of 'truthiness' as 'Tony Blair saying: "British troops in Iraq are only facing resistance from some fierce insurgents" when some would argue the reality is of a country... on the brink of a civil war.'

And finally, a profound insight from Professor Richard Dawkins, who reminds us that: 'Human suffering has been caused because too many of us cannot grasp that words are only tools for our use.'

FINAL THOUGHTS ON 'IMPROPAGANDA'

This analysis of 'impropaganda' is not meant to amount to a moral justification of the practice. It seeks to demonstrate an aspect of creativity that is used – or, indeed, some may say abused – in promotional work. In practising 'impropaganda', the opportunistic publicist is in danger of compromising the long-term

brand values of the organization he or she represents. The public relations practitioner, in contrast, is seeking to uphold the organization's long-term brand values.

On a personal level, practitioners who admit in private to practising what amounts to 'impropaganda' are people who operate within high standards of personal ethics in what they define as the essential values and issues in life. They tend to be true to themselves, true to their friends and true to their concept of truth. Their acts of 'impropaganda' are cushioned with views that such action is undertaken without hurting anyone or compromising a major issue in society, such as the state of the health service. Neither should it be used in a real-life crisis or issue of genuine importance. It is seemingly a game played in 'tabloid space', where no one gets hurt and both parties get what they want from the relationship. On one side of the equation, journalistic licence is employed by the media to create good stories, and on the other side the equivalent creative licence for the publicist is used to supply the relevant fix for the journalist. It is a world where, rather like Father Christmas, fantasy is clinically bottled and marketed, but where make-believe has strayed into mainstream news.

On a professional level, however, there is serious concern about the need to uphold the integrity and status of public relations practice. The Chartered Institute of Public Relations, in its Code of Practice, makes it clear that members should conduct their professional activities with proper regard to the public interest. They should have a positive duty to observe the highest standards in the practice of public relations and to deal fairly and honestly with all public audiences, including those reached through the media of communications.

This chapter does not seek to condone certain creative practices, but it recognizes that a greater understanding of some of the skills associated with our profession cannot be achieved by an act of denial, or wishing that something should not be true. That in itself may, of course, be an act of 'impropaganda'!

SUMMARY

1. Contriving the facts or the objective focus of a situation can creatively produce short-term added value but with risk to long-term credibility.

2. The opportunistic publicist may compromise long-term brand values for short-term gain. The public relations practitioner will work to uphold long-term brand values.
3. To protect the status and integrity of the profession, the Institute of Public Relations has a detailed Code of Practice, with which all members have to comply.
4. Ralph Waldo Emerson once wrote: 'The louder a man talks about honour, the quicker I count the spoons.'
5. A final thought. Most popular historical 'fact' is, on closer study, the product of 'impropaganda'.

KEY WORDS FOR YOUR CREATIVITY VOCABULARY

- Impropaganda.
- Punk PR.
- Shock PR.

16

The future of creativity

Tomorrow, tomorrow,
I like tomorrow,
The flowers are growing.

A poem by Lizzie Green, aged seven

An implicit belief in this book is that creativity plays a crucial role in today's public relations work. What, however, of the future? What developments are likely to take place either to diminish or to develop the creative role in public relations? Even without a crystal ball, it is possible to use creative tools and understanding of the creative process to identify a number of trends and issues.

THE CREATIVE RANGE

Using the Creative Range technique (explained in Chapter 5), it is possible to establish the parameters of future scenarios for creativity in public relations. The Safe Bet Option can be best demonstrated by a comment from the late Professor Michael

Balfour: 'The basic principle... is that publicity is a function of policy, not something that can be treated separately and decided after everything else has been arranged'. This would seem to be at the forefront of current thinking about involving the public relations practitioner at the heart of strategy and policy. Yet it was written in 1947, in Balfour's former role as Chief of Information at the Board of Trade. So, at one end of the Creative Range, the Safe Bet Option is the scenario of nothing much changing; thus the current uncertainties about what is creativity, its role, and how you go about being creative, could continue to shroud the subject.

At the other end of the Creative Range, the Extreme Option, practitioners may require a professional qualification – the Creative Licence – in order to practise. This will demonstrate that they have a full understanding of creativity, the creative process, knowledge of the leading-edge techniques and tips on creating ideas, and how to apply them in what used to be called public relations. And pigs might fly.

What are the future trends and developments between these two extreme scenarios and how are they likely to affect how we go about being creative? Set out below are some of my suggestions. The different stages of the creative process – the five 'I's of Information, Incubation, Integration, Illumination and Illustration (see Chapter 4) – are all set to be transformed by how practitioners apply themselves to each.

THE INFORMATION STAGE TRANSFORMED

Significant progress is likely to be made in reducing the number of ill-structured tasks in public relations. The use of technology may enable practitioners to call up computer-generated scenarios, with ready-made solutions to the problem faced. Green Light thinking skills, to provide new insights for defining a problem or coming up with a solution, will only be used should the computer models prove unsatisfactory.

Competition between all companies will, in the future, be more intensive as a result of the emergence of global markets, rapid technological developments, and the increased rate of change in consumer tastes. The companies of tomorrow are likely to succeed in minimizing the difference between them, not only in their means of production but also in hygiene factors, such as matching

each other's service levels. Greater emphasis will therefore be placed on their market differentiation, namely how they are able to manage their image and present a perception of a distinction between themselves and their competitors. Indeed, it could be argued that the only companies that will survive in the future are the ones with a clear focus and a clear differentiation from their rivals.

Crucial to this task of differentiation is a clear positioning for the successful organization (see Chapter 9). As a result, there is an outstanding opportunity for creative public relations practitioners to be at the centre of their organization's strategic and policy development, but contributing to the definition and updating of the organization's positioning.

With the increasingly rapid rate of change, there will be scope for the creative practitioner to help organizations not only to face up to the problems of today, but also to anticipate and contribute to the challenges of tomorrow, by creating a better understanding of the future. At present, successful organizations are those that can either best anticipate future trends, or at least have the flexibility to respond swiftly and effectively to new opportunities. The challenge for the future will increasingly be one of timing; as a result of the increased rate of change, 'tomorrow' will be coming much sooner.

Organizations will need to improve their abilities in what can be called 'the anticipation of the next'. This will help them move even more swiftly to identify opportunities and capitalize upon the value created by any new developments. The creative practitioner can help to redefine information not as knowledge from past experience, but as half-emerged truths that need to be monitored and tracked as they emerge as the facts of tomorrow. This redefinition of information as being of the future as well as of the past will be coupled to the harnessing, for future scenario planning, of many of the creative thinking techniques described in this book. No longer will this area of work be the province of the organization's corporate planners; the creative public relations practitioner has an opportunity to move the centre of corporate strategy and policy making.

The information revolution continues

The task of obtaining information for briefing purposes is being

revolutionized. Through the internet, practitioners are already benefiting from new sources of knowledge and being exposed to a far wider range of materials.

In a positive scenario, this trend of open sources of information is likely to develop, with ever more sophisticated forms of internet access and storage of data. When faced with a new creative task, practitioners will enter in their key information requirements. Rather than instantly receiving a huge volume of data about the subject, the computer (or whatever equipment may replace it), could instead present the material in a structured format so as to assist the practitioner's management of the information. This information could be presented in a number of ways, ranging from 'essential to know for the task' to 'wacky way-out variables offering potential for further creative treatment'.

A pessimistic future scenario may depict development of greater ownership, control, and restrictions on the use of certain key pieces of knowledge. The emergence of 'Infopreneurs' – people wielding control over branded information – could limit the availability of information. The potential to employ creativity to overcome difficulties in gaining access, or alternatives to branded information, may be a distinguishing feature of the creative practitioner of the future.

The problem of 'information fatigue' may also emerge. You can probably relate to what can be labelled the 'Vivaldi syndrome'; an outstanding creative work (in this case, classical music) is heard in a wide variety of out-of-context uses, such as on call-waiting telephone systems or in television commercials, which results in its appreciation being devalued. In researching this book, a large number of the same quotes, anecdotes and analogies used by writers of management textbooks have been found; consequently, there is a danger of these so-called pearls of wisdom appearing stale and tired through their constant reuse and misuse. The challenge to creative practitioners will be to identify new sources of material so that their communications are fresh and original.

An area of great potential development in the study of public relations is the history of our industry itself, together with the numerous case studies and examples of outstanding practice that it contains. There is a tendency to think only of current public relations practice offering relevant and valid experiences for our work. Yet studying historical material – whether Professor Balfour's *Propaganda 1939–45*, or reading up on the exploits in the 19th

century of the great showman Barnum – can provide a wealth of information for today's practitioners to apply in new contexts. It was once said that the only thing that history teaches us is that we do not learn from history. But there is a fund of creative ideas in public relations history.

THE INCUBATION STAGE TRANSFORMED

The biggest challenge facing the understanding of creativity and the creative process is greater knowledge of the incubation process, where the brain takes in certain information and at a later time produces an illumination. The human mind remains largely unexplored. What is the process at work inside our heads during the Incubation stage? What exactly goes on in people's brains for ideas to emerge and for some people to be outstandingly creative and others less so? What are the constituent elements of an idea that give it potential to develop and later emerge as a creative idea?

There are so many questions. The future has the potential to provide the answers and then be harnessed by creative practitioners.

THE ILLUMINATION STAGE TRANSFORMED

There is no doubt that with greater understanding of the creative processes there will be recognition by individuals and organizations of the need to capture and harness our illuminations – the ideas our brains are constantly producing (and most probably failing to record).

Increased understanding of the techniques and tips described in this book to stimulate Green Light thinking will take place. Brainstorming and 'awayday' sessions will be scheduled as routine activities, rather than the present tendency of taking place when there is a problem, or when someone has an illumination of the need to spend some time specifically being creative.

Technology may provide recording devices such as watches with a microphone and digital recording facility. The intensity of the desire to capture any outstanding Green Light thinking may be such that, along with a greater availability of recording devices for

individual use, every room in a building in the future could contain facilities for recording our illuminations.

Coupled with the ability to capture illuminations will be the extension of facilities to store these ideas, in the form of words, images or sounds. Computers will be able to manage and manipulate this vast store of Green Light thinking, so as to enable the creative practitioner to work to optimum efficiency.

In addition to technology gearing itself to harnessing illuminations, working practices will also adapt to this requirement. Formal meetings may feature illumination breaks, recognizing that the brains of participants at a meeting are capable not just of functioning on the agenda at hand but on a host of other tasks. 'Excuse me while I record an illumination' may be a common phrase of the 21st century. What is certain is the tremendous scope to improve the efficiency of the Illumination stage for the creative practitioner of the future.

THE INTEGRATION STAGE TRANSFORMED

Public relations practice has been revolutionized over the last decade. The typical public relations office at the beginning of the 1990s would have had just one computer for up to a dozen people. Nowadays the computer is an indispensable personal tool. It has only been since the 1990s that the availability of mobile phones has become widespread. During the 1990s, the fax machine, without which working life was once unthinkable, began to be supplanted by computer modems.

Creative practitioners will in the future be able to make use of a whole new array of advances in computer-based scenario planning, idea permutation software, media monitoring and targeting, computer-enhanced photography – all of them able to assist in developing creative ideas. If you think you have seen a technological revolution over the last 10 years, you ain't seen nothing yet.

In the Integration stage, six key elements are likely to provide a greater source of added value in the creative dimension of public relations work. These six are:

Creating contacts

New challenges are emerging to face the public relations

practitioner. The task, for example, of dealing with the media is being made more difficult, with fewer journalists being employed.

An increasingly frustrating aspect of media relations is how journalists are becoming more remote. They are less likely to come along to events, or make site visits, as a result of the fewer staff employed and increased pressures on their time. Even getting through on the phone can be extremely difficult, with increasing use of answer machines or secretaries who deal with any approach by 'faxwalling' – 'Can you send your story by fax or e-mail?'

Creative public relations practitioners will be looking to use their creative skills to overcome this problem, which is likely to get worse in the future.

Creating ready-made options

Technology can be employed in idea-generating techniques to provide a large number of readily available ideas for practitioners to use. Software capable of producing forced combinations, such as the Matrix Technique (explained in Chapter 5) will be used for instantly generating large numbers of permutations – useful, for example, when considering ideas for a photocall.

Creating legends

One area that practitioners do not currently fully exploit is the building, or creating, of 'legends' for their organizations or clients.

Most successful companies have a number of examples of outstanding customer service or of achievements. Working in tandem with the organization's positioning, these company 'legends' will be used to translate the organization's values and visions into behaviours that other people – their employees, partners and customers – can readily understand and identify with. These people present an exceptional opportunity for the creative practitioner to differentiate clearly between organizations, which can then be communicated to different audiences.

Creating metaphors

To stand out in a communications marketplace of information overload, the creative practitioner will be looking – like the

postman who became a poet in the Italian film *Il Postino* – to make use of metaphors.

In Neuro Linguistic Programming, metaphors are recognized to work on at least two levels in communications. On a conscious level the metaphor is what it seems – a story or fable. However, on a second level it allows us to talk to the subconscious mind in such a way that the conscious mind cannot censor or reject the underlying message. The campaign metaphor could be a standard part of the communications programme of the future, as creative practitioners seek to relate their message in new levels of understanding and insight.

Creating traditions

The British tourism trade is fortunate in being able to capitalize on many age-old traditions, such as the Changing of the Guard at Buckingham Palace. Yet no matter how old some of these traditions are, they all started at some time or another. A fruitful area of the public relations campaign of the future is actually to create a new tradition.

All traditions have to start some day, so why not start new ones to carry on into the future beyond the 21st century?

Creating words

As children, we are told that 'sticks and stones may break my bones, but names will never hurt me'. The adage should have had an additional sentence (not exactly scanning!) that goes on: '… but names can also be a very effective public relations tool'. Creating new words or names can help provide a more accurate definition and label to use in any public relations debate. In the future, changes in technology and tastes will require more specific terminology in order to avoid potential confusion.

As future life gets more complex, there is likely to be a tendency for individuals to relate increasingly to subsets, or subgroups, within the wider society. One way that these subgroups will mark themselves out is by developing and acquiring their own distinctive terminology and vocabulary. This trend will be mirrored by organizations also acquiring their own set of jargon to mark themselves out to the rest of the world, and to act as a unifying force for members of the subgroup. In this context, the creative practitioner

can make a significant contribution by inventing new words, or redefining or developing existing terms, to use in public relations campaigns.

This book contains a number of potential neologisms, for example 'impropaganda', 'faxwalling' and 'incubation rest'. These could gain wider currency if they help to create greater understanding, or are seen by relevant audiences (or significant others) to add value to communication. The public relations campaigns of the future may well include the creative dimension of creating new words as an inherent part of the programme.

THE ILLUSTRATION STAGE TRANSFORMED

There is no doubt that creative practitioners are likely to become more skilled in the Illustration stage of the creative process, with a greater knowledge of the specific skills and techniques required in the successful selling of ideas to gain acceptance by decision makers.

Techniques providing computer simulations of how public relations programmes will appear – virtual PR campaigns – will be used. When you consider how the once state-of-the-art computer-simulated software used in the film *Toy Story* is now affordable for use on the home computer, in the space of just three years, present-day facilities for presentation must soon appear antiquated.

AND FINALLY: GREATER STUDY OF CREATIVITY

This book has, it is hoped, made a useful start in the study and understanding of creativity in public relations. If defines creativity, explains how we go about being creative and how to manage the creative dimension as individuals and organizations. No longer the Cinderella of public relations study, creativity is ripe for more research. Creativity as a skill is now an evident fact of life for effective public relations practice.

In conclusion, a thought: whether it is the practice of public relations or the state of the world in general, the only way for the

flowers to grow tomorrow – to make tomorrow better than today – is by more creativity.

KEY WORDS FOR YOUR CREATIVITY VOCABULARY

- Legends.
- Metaphors.

17

Award ceremony

Congratulations. You have now completed *Creativity in Public Relations*. As an instructed reader you should possess:

- a working definition of creativity to guide you in your work;
- an understanding of the nature of creativity;
- an awareness of the creative process and how to manage it to optimum effect;
- knowledge of Green Light and Red Light thinking, and when (and when not) to use them;
- a way of overcoming obstacles that limit your creative abilities;
- an appreciation of the ingredients making up the creative individual and creative organization;
- a distinction between the creative publicist and the creative public relations practitioner; and
- an insight into future developments that are likely to affect creativity.

Now present yourself with your Creative Licence. Impress your friends and colleagues. Go forth and be creative.

Creative Licence

Awarded to:

You

This is to certify that having read 'Creativity in Public Relations' you can be a more creative practitioner.

Figure 17.1 *Your Creative Licence*

18

Interested in finding out more?

Picasso was once reputed to have appeared on Spanish television and produced a painting in several minutes. When the television presenter was told that this new work would be worth several thousand pounds, he remonstrated with the artist, saying: 'How can you justify something costing this much for just a few minutes work?' To which Picasso replied: 'This hasn't taken me a few minutes. It's taken a lifetime.'

This book is the product of a lifetime's experiences. The books and contacts below may help develop further your understanding of creativity. They will not only increase your knowledge but should also provide a lot of enjoyment.

FAVOURITE BOOKS ON CREATIVITY AND DEVELOPING YOUR MIND'S CREATIVE SKILLS

● John Adair, *Effective Innovation* (1996) Pan, London. This book is a good general guide to the topic of creativity.

- Silvano Arieti, *Creativity, the Magic Synthesis* (1976) Basic Books, USA. This is useful on creativity's historical development.
- Tony Buzan, *Buzan's Book of Genius* (1994) Stanley Paul, London. This book is extremely good and combines mind skills with numerous historical biographics. If you are pushed for time, his *Superself* (1997) Gower, Aldershot, produced in a cartoon format, is good fun.
- Edward de Bono has written extensively on creativity. My favourite is his *Textbook of Wisdom* (1997) Penguin, Harmondsworth, written in just four mornings. The afternoons were apparently too hot. For his ideas on lateral thinking, read *The Use of Lateral Thinking* (1990), Penguin, Harmondsworth.
- Peter Evans and Geoff Deehan, *The Keys to Creativity* (1990) Grafton, London. This gives a good overview.
- Michael Michalko, *Thinkertoys* (1991) Ten Speed Press, Berkeley. Probably the best book on techniques.
- Alex Osborn, *Applied Imagination* (1953) Creative Education Foundations Press, New York. This may come across as dated in its style, but it is a seminal work in promoting the management of the creative process in marketing.
- Roger von Oeuch, *A Whack on the Side of the Head* (1992) Warner Books. This book contains some great quotes and metaphors.
- Robert Weisberg, *Creativity Beyond the Myth of Genius* (1993) Freeman, New York. This one is interesting for highlighting the incremental nature of creativity.

BOOKS ON CREATIVITY IN MARKETING

- Winston Fletcher is an excellent writer on marketing. My personal favourite is *How to Capture the Advertising High Ground* (1994) Century, London.
- Guy Kawasaki, *How to Drive Your Competition Crazy* (1995) Hyperion, New York. This book offers an alternative insight into modern-day marketing and business.
- Professor Simon Majaro of Cranfield School of Management, *Managing Ideas for Profit* (1992) McGraw-Hill, Maidenhead.
- Regis McKenna, *Relationship Marketing* (1991) Addison-Wesley, Reading, MA. This gives a useful insight into creative marketing in a fast-moving environment.

- David Ogilvy, *Advertising* (1987) Prion, London. This is, rightly, one of the best-loved books in marketing.

BOOKS ON CREATIVITY IN ORGANIZATIONS

- Min Basudur, *Innovation* (1995) Pitman, London. This gives an excellent analysis of approaches to problem solving and processes for change within organizations.
- R Meredith Belbin, *Team Roles at Work* (1997) Butterworth-Heinemann, Oxford. This is a good practical guide to team building.
- John Kao, *Jamming* (1996) HarperCollins, London. This offers valuable insights into how businesses should harness creativity.
- There is an extensive choice of material from Tom Peters on how businesses can face up to the challenges of modern-day life. My personal favourite is *A Passion for Excellence* (1996) Fontana, London.

BOOKS ON SELF-DEVELOPMENT

- In Dale Carnegie's *How to Win Friends and Influence People* or *How to Stop Worrying and Start Living* (1952) Chancellor Press, London – and even though the titles may be a shade self-conscious and the style dated – the lessons remain timeless for understanding what motivates people.
- Stephen Covey, *The Seven Habits of Highly Effective People* (1989) Simon & Schuster, London. This book provides a good model and framework for fine-tuning your individual skills and motivations.
- Rex Johnson and David Swindley, *Decide to Win* (1996) Ward Lock, London. This book provides an insight into motivation in sports psychology, which can be used to improve both your serve in tennis and your all-round creativity.
- Graham Lancaster, *The 20% Factor* (1993) Kogan Page, London. This is a good guide to self-improvement.

NEURO LINGUISTIC PROGRAMMING

- Joseph O'Connor and John Seymour, *Training with NLP* (1994) Thorsons, London. This book provides a readable introduction to a subject that will play an increasingly important role in the way we approach communications.

INTERNET SITES

These change rapidly, so make sure you perform regular searches. My favourite sites include:

- The Australian-based Creativity Web which can be found at www.ozemail.com.au/~caveman/creative/.
- Learn to live each day as your birthday at peterrussell.com. Includes a feature that calculates the number of days you have been alive.
- The innovation network at thinksmart.com has a range of articles on creativity and innovation.

TRAINING COURSES

- The Chartered Institute of Public Relations runs a wide range of courses for the professional development of practitioners, including 'Improving your Creativity'. For further details telephone +44 (0) 20 7253 5151.
- A range of creativity training courses using the material in this book is available from GREEN communications, telephone +44 (0) 1924 363222; Web site: creativityatwork.co.uk.
- For courses on beliefs and values, the 'New Ways of Thinking' workshop run by Steve McDermott of McDermott & Associates is highly recommended. Telephone +44 (0) 1132 860022.
- A growing number of higher education institutions is running courses on creativity or innovation. Check your local university for any relevant courses.

ORGANIZATIONS

- If you are not a member of the Chartered Institute of Public Relations, then do become one. Also, highly recommended for qualified practitioners is the Public Relations Society of America.
- The Leo Lunch is a celebration held during the sign of Leo every year. It recognizes that many of the country's outstanding creative public relations practitioners are born under the astrological sign of Leo (which, of course, is a very Leo thing to say). For further details please contact The Remembrancer, Douglas Smith of Westminster Advisers, on +44 (0) 20 7222 9500.

Index